ACKNO\

I wish to acknowledge and thank:

Andie Newell, for her prayerful insights, constructive feedback, and continuous support. I don't know what I would do without you.

Connie Mitchell, for her careful editing, for finding my seemingly ever-present errors in Scripture references (who can figure?), and for her enthusiasm over the project.

Susan and Taylor Field, for their willingness to read and go out on a limb to endorse my work. Everything you've accomplished for the Kingdom in your life leaves me in awe—and inspired.

Naomi Craig, for her positivity, encouragement, willingness to help, and overall excitement for life. Thanks for being my critique partner.

Hayden Lane, for providing me a continual stream of resources offering me a variety of perspectives on Christian faith and for being willing to challenge me.

Lindsey Lane, for uplifting my spirits and bringing me so much joy.

And most of all, David Lane, for his unyielding love and support, his patience with the process, and his willingness to offer endless encouragement in all areas of my life, not just in my writing. You are my Solid, my Forever, and my Split-apart.

DEDICATION

4

To David

with whom I share and will share a Kingdom dwelling.

TABLE OF CONTENTS

CHAPTER ONE
THE JOURNEY TO YOUR DWELLING

Your life is the story of a journey—a journey toward a specific destination. You choose the whole of your journey. You create its substance, its nature, and its quality. Your story is written by a series of choices—your choices. Even when other characters in the story or circumstances beyond your choice influence your journey, you are able to choose your feelings and responses to those events and set your course forward from there. Each and every choice, from the largest to the most seemingly insignificant, affects your experience of the story.

Imagine yourself setting out on a path. Step by step, the path develops before you, shaped by your footfalls. It winds through pleasant green fields dotted with splashes of color and the fresh fragrance of earth and flowers. Another step, and it twists and turns into dark jungles whose vines threaten to entangle you and whose quicksand tries to engulf you, then empties into a valley filled with shadow. It bursts out onto open sand and the cleansing smell of salt air, only to dive into deep caverns from which you fear there is no escape. With another step, you reach a thick forest trail winding up the side of a mountain. The view from the top is spectacular.

You have this certainty at the outset of the journey—a piece of good news to encourage you along the way. Jesus has gone before you. He has prepared a special destination, a dwelling He's created just for you. He also journeys with you. He knows the way, and He wants to take you there. He said so Himself.

"There are many dwelling places in my Father's house. Otherwise, I would have told you, because I am going away to make ready a place for you. And if I go and make ready a place for you, I will come again and take you to be with me, so that where I am you may be too" (John 14:2-3 NET).

You've also been told certain things about your destination. Somewhere up ahead, beyond the fields, jungles, valleys, beaches, caverns, and mountains, unseen by your eyes, is a magnificent dwelling place, fit for the child of a King and built in the land of the Father. The splendor, majesty, glory, strength, abundance, and joy found in this dwelling place has been described to you in detail (I Chronicles 16:27-28, Psalm 26:8, Psalm 36:8-9, Psalm 84:1, Psalm 91:1, Revelation 21:1-4, 10-11).

Despite all you've been told about the destination, the nature of your journey continues to be enigmatic. Your story unfolds on multiple dimensions. One aspect takes you into the deep places within you where Jesus prepares an internal dwelling to share with you. This journey is about revelation and healing, but it's also a journey of relationship and connection, wisdom and understanding, and above all, love. Another part of your story takes you step by step and choice by choice to the heavenly dwelling Jesus has prepared for you. This journey is one of sanctification, maturation, and holiness.

These two dimensions are concurrent, parallel passages leading to different understandings of one destination. They both lead to the Kingdom of God; however, they lead to different yet coexisting experiences of the Kingdom.

The first journey seeks to expose and clear out the tangled vines and quicksand of your inner jungle and pull you from your cave or hiding place, and to bring truth where it's needed. The goal is to free you for an abundant life *now* in your internal dwelling—the Kingdom of God within your heart.

When Jesus came, He brought the Kingdom of God with Him. He preached about the Kingdom of God's contemporaneous presence several times (Mark 1:15, 9:1, Luke 9:27, 10:9-11, 11:20). In response to a question about when the Kingdom of God would come, He replied, "The coming of the kingdom of God is not something that can be observed, nor will people say, 'Here it is,' or 'There it is,' because the kingdom of God is in your midst." (Luke 17:20-21).

Now, because of Jesus' death and resurrection and the presence of the Holy Spirit living in your heart, the Kingdom of God is within you (another possible translation of Luke 17:21). Yes, you carry God's Kingdom inside you. You live in the Kingdom of God *now.* The division between the temporal and the eternal—between earth and heaven—has been torn asunder in you, just as the veil of the Temple was ripped from top to bottom. You no longer make a distinction between this physical life and your heavenly life. You no longer wait for the Kingdom. When Jesus took up residence, you became a Kingdom citizen and stepped into eternal life, and your journey to your heavenly dwelling began.

This journey seeks to teach you to walk in alignment with Jesus toward "being transformed into His image" (II Corinthians 3:18), in preparation for your arrival at your dwelling in heaven. Nothing of this world—no lie, nothing spoiled or tainted by sin, nothing connected to evil—can enter the Kingdom of heaven. This is why your body must die before you go to heaven. Your body is still connected to this world and tainted by sin. As Paul describes, "For the perishable must clothe itself with the imperishable, and the mortal with immortality" (I Corinthians 15:53).

Likewise, anything within you not of His Kingdom must perish before you reach your heavenly dwelling. Your transformational journey with Jesus draws you ever closer to your dwelling place. But when you step out on your own, away from the leading of Jesus, you hinder your journey toward holiness.

Matthew chapters 5 and 6 talk at some length about who receives the Kingdom of heaven, who will see God, and who will be called children of God. Some interpret these verses as outlining what we have to do to be saved, but Scripture is clear that, "If you declare with your mouth, 'Jesus is Lord' and believe in your heart that God raised him from the dead, you will be saved (Romans 10:9), and, "Everyone who calls on the name of the Lord will be saved" (Romans 10:13), so these verses refer to some other kind of receiving the Kingdom beyond salvation. They refer to the qualities of holiness, like humility, purity, peace, and righteousness which are requirements for your heavenly dwelling.

Matthew 18:2-3 and Matthew 19:14 present another requirement for entering the Kingdom of heaven—to become like little children—but once again, Jesus isn't referring to salvation in this teaching. He is describing a process of becoming. This process is a restorative one, bringing you back to your original creation, your identity given to you at your inception. Like so many things in God's Kingdom, His process is counterintuitive to the world's perception of becoming. Rather than growing up, you are to grow back and return to your earlier state—be born again—back before so many things of the world covered over your identity. To be spiritually mature, you must become like a child.

When Jesus speaks about receiving the Kingdom, I believe Jesus is describing your maturation process along the journey. Your eternal path starts when you receive Jesus as your Lord and Savior, but that is the beginning, not the end of the journey. During the journey, you grow toward becoming poor in spirit, pure in heart, a peacemaker, and radically righteous. You develop a deep desire to live God's commands—love God and love your neighbor as yourself (Matthew 22:37-39). Your heart moves toward love even for your enemies. You lose your desire to receive recognition or praise from others for the good things you do. You become more and more like little children. Above all, you "store up for yourselves treasures in heaven...for where your treasure is, there your *heart* will be also" (Matthew 6:20-21).

The passage to holiness must be walked to reach your Kingdom dwelling, as Jesus indicates in these teachings. But it's unlikely you will have reached full maturation in all these areas by the end of your physical life. When you arrive in heaven, you may be far along the passage leading to your heavenly dwelling, or you may still have some distance to go. In any case, the maturation process to holiness *will be walked* in its entirety, whether this process takes place on earth or in heaven.

Those who have walked farther on earth are "rewarded" with a shorter journey to their dwelling place with Jesus—they enter heaven closer to the experience of the full glory of their Kingdom dwelling. Those who have stored up treasures on earth will have to shed the worldly things they've clung to, because those things have no place in your heavenly dwelling, but those who have stored up treasures in heaven will already have those treasures to enjoy in their dwelling place. The bottom line is what you choose on earth has implications for your experience in heaven. *Your choices matter.*

Ancient Journeys

Psalm 107 chronicles the many journeys of the Lord's people, from those who wandered in desert wastelands to those in the darkness in prison chains to the afflicted because of their foolish, rebellious ways to those whose courage failed during times of peril. About each journey, the psalmist says, "He delivered them/saved them/brought them out" in some manner (v. 6, 13, 19, 28). What is interesting is the manner of His rescues: "He led them by a straight way to a city where they could settle" (v. 7); "He brought them out of darkness, the utter darkness, and broke away their chains" (v. 14); "He sent out His word and healed them; He rescued them from the grave" (v. 20); "He stilled the storm to a whisper, the waves of the sea were hushed...and He guided them to their desired haven" (v. 29-30).

Do you see the different ways God led the people on journeys from the place their self-determined choices landed them to another place (a city, a haven) to redeem them from their distress? Do you see the ways He brought healing to their hearts (breaking their chains, sending out His word, quieting the storm)?

I've always believed Israel's story is a reflection of our story. In other words, the paths we walk, the struggles we have, and the ways God intervenes on our behalf mirror what we read about God's people in the Old Testament. We make their same mistakes. We have their same dense stubbornness—what Scripture calls being stiff-necked. We quickly forget what God has done for us and what He's taught us and turn to lies and other, false gods in our lives. These choices leave us in the same distress as the children of Israel.

So, I read these verses and see a direct reflection of our parallel passages to the Kingdom of God—both within our hearts and in heaven. I see how God takes us by the hand and leads us to another destination, our dwelling place, and in the process frees us from our chains and heals us. As the psalmist says, "Let the one who is wise heed these things and ponder the loving deeds of the Lord" (v. 43).

Diverging Paths

A third dimension of your journey presents as a dichotomy of possible paths leading to very different outcomes. As you read in Psalm 107, each aspect of the story begins with some choice or choices that took the people down a wrong road, to their destruction. They wandered (v. 4), they rebelled (v. 11, 17), they despised God's ways (v. 11), they stumbled (v. 12), they became fools (v. 17), they sinned (v. 17), they gave into fear (v. 26-27). Then, God comes in response to their cries and guides them down another path to redemption.

Like Israel, you are presented diverging paths as choices. Jesus described the two different kinds of paths laid before you as wide or narrow—one type easy and spacious, and one difficult—one type leading to destruction, and the other leading to life and dwelling with the King. (Matthew 7:13-14). It's up to you to choose from the infinite options available on both kinds of paths.

The wide, easy paths are, first and foremost, *familiar.* Because they are familiar, they feel comfortable and safe to you. Our society defines, encourages, and accepts these pathways. As a result, these paths are also *well-established.* Many have walked on them before you. Their undergrowth is tamped down, and their course is already trampled and worn, making the paths appear flat and effortless. The generations before you may have walked these kinds of paths, and if so, they begin early in your life showing you the way. Walking these paths may become *habit* as much as choice by the time you are old enough to start deciding your own course.

Before you start out, you know where the wide paths lead, because others are glad to show you, reflected in their lives, and you have plenty of examples to highlight their potential destinations. Power, control, security, self-gratification, acceptance, avoidance of pain—these are the things often sought on the wide roads, although most people might not identify those concepts as determining their course.

Although the destinations along these wide paths may appear enticing, they are also *transient* and as fleeting as a wisp of cloud, or they are *illusory*. The author of Ecclesiastes describes it this way: "What benefit do people get from all the effort which they expend on earth? The eye is never satisfied with seeing, nor is the ear ever content with hearing. What exists now is what will be, and what has been done is what will be done; there is truly nothing new on earth. Everything...is *hebel* (the Hebrew word here, *hebel*, means transitory or fleeting)—like chasing the wind" (1:3, 8-9, 14 NET).

The narrow ways are nothing like the wide roads. They aren't well-worn; in fact, they are often barely visible or so overgrown you're not sure where to take the next step. You have few examples of those who've walked them well, and the ultimate destination can only be seen by faith through spiritual eyes. They can be *risky* and *lonely* paths.

The narrow paths are *radical*. Society doesn't accept them and often ridicules them as ignorant, foolish, abnormal, or crazy. These paths can lead through deep valleys, through raging storms, beside steep precipices, and over high ridges. They appear *unsafe*. They promise much suffering and hardship with no guarantee of relief until you reach heaven.

On top of that, the ultimate destination is an unknown to all except those who are already there. Vaguely described through symbolism and metaphor, you're left to imagine what the destination you're struggling so hard to reach will be like, and you find you can't imagine it. You're asked to accept on faith that the destination is worth the journey.

Your motivations along the narrow ways also have nothing in common with the things sought on the wide roads. Instead of power and control, you value freedom (Galatians 5:1). Instead of security, you receive truth as your protection and peace as the guard over your heart and mind (Philippians 4:7). Self-gratification is replaced by joy (Psalm 16:11), and acceptance is replaced by love (Romans 5:5). Suffering is no longer feared but is used for its benefits of producing righteousness, perseverance, character, and hope within you (Hebrews 12:11; Romans 5:3-4). These gains are not wisps of cloud blown away on the first breath of wind but are lasting anchors in your life once they are gained through a process of developing deep relationship with Jesus. Be warned—these anchors are hard-won.

So, there are your choices. You have a virtually endless string of wide paths and countless narrow paths before you. Each and every choice you make sets your feet on a course. Every thought, every feeling, every action, every decision takes you in a direction. Every choice matters.

It's a bit overwhelming, isn't it?

The Boat and the Dock

I love riding on boats, particularly fast boats where I can sit on the bow, holding onto the rail, with the wind in my hair and mist from the waves the boat makes plowing through the waters coating me. It feels like pure joy. But getting on the boat is another matter. I'll stand on the dock, looking at that leap down onto the rocking deck, shifting from foot to foot, insecure about taking that step. In my imagination, I see the boat pushing away from the dock as I set my first foot down, and my legs splitting too far apart, resulting in me falling with a loud splash into the water.

The truth is, you can't stand with one foot on the deck and one on the dock. You just can't do it. You must risk the plunge and step out in faith that the boat will be there for both of your feet.

It's interesting that, for me, stepping back onto the dock doesn't feel insecure. The dock isn't moving like the boat in the water. It's set and stable—or so it seems, compared to the boat. So, I step right up, no worries and no hesitation.

I like it when my husband steps down into the boat before me and reaches his hand up for me to hold as I step down onto the deck. I feel confident then.

The Kingdom path is like the boat. It won't be tied down. It doesn't appear stable or safe. It's wild and reckless and radical and free and filled with joy and pleasure. Jesus is the husband, the One who goes before and reaches out with the helping hand.

The dock is the world. It gives the appearance of solidity but it's actually a rickety old wooden structure with no real foundation. A good wave sends it bouncing and reeling. In fact, when a wave of substance comes, the dock bangs against the harbored boats, causing damage. It has cracks and splinters and ultimately disintegrates in the light of the sun. It has nothing for you—no joy or pleasure or excitement, just a broad, flat place to wait.

You cannot stand with one foot in the world and one in the Kingdom. You must go all-in and take the leap, with both feet firmly planted in the Kingdom way. For if you step back on the dock, you *will* plant your feet there, which sends you down the wide road to your destruction.

To continue the analogy, once you've ridden on a boat for a while, stepping back onto the dock is disorienting. The ground feels unsteady and your steps wobbly. This is another reason for keeping both feet on the boat (in the Kingdom) and not falling into the trap of stepping back onto the dock (the worldly way) where it's easy for you to fall.

Your choices are your steps, with each step landing in the boat or on the dock—in the Kingdom or in the world. And each step furthers your journey in some direction toward some destination. The question for you to ask as you choose is: Will this choice lead me closer to the Kingdom or send me further away?

Which Way to Go?

After Jesus shared with the disciples that He was going away to prepare a place for them, and that He would come back and take them to be with Him, He said, "And you know the way where I am going" (John 14:4 NET), much to the consternation of a confused (and often maligned) Thomas, who pointed out, "Lord, we don't know where you are going. How can we know the way?" (John 14:5 NET).

Poor Thomas. He gets a bad rap as the doubter in Jesus' story, but he asks a valid question. He can't see the path laid out before him. He doesn't know the destination. He's never been to the Father's house (at least, not that he recalls). So, why does Jesus think he can choose the right path and find the way?

Jesus' response to Thomas is simple and infinitely profound. "I am the way, and the truth, and the life. No one comes to the Father except through me" (John 14:6 NET).

I know you've heard that verse repeatedly, and it's probably become rote to you by now, like the Lord's prayer or John 3:16, and may have lost some of its import as a result. But let's take a moment to unpack it and see if there's something in it you've missed. First, remember Jesus is answering Thomas' question, so his response addresses, "How can we know the way?" Essentially, Jesus is acknowledging you don't know the way. You can't—*unless* you know *Him*. Go back to John 14:3— "I will come again and *take you* to be with me." He then follows up with, "And you know the way where I am going." Jesus wasn't suggesting the disciples were on their own to find their way. The disciples knew Jesus; *therefore*, they knew the way, because they knew *Him*.

Jesus' discourse on making ready your place in His Father's house is much more than information on the future. It's instruction for the present.

You are not supposed to walk the narrow path alone. Otherwise, in all honesty, who would choose it? Stumbling along in darkness without clear direction, creeping along the edge of cliffs where one misstep means plummeting into the depths, facing howling storms and crashing waves without knowing how or where to sail? Knowing those things, most would say, "No, thank you."

Most *do* say, "No, thank you," because they don't know the Guide.

Jesus is saying the *only way* to get to the Father's dwelling place is with Him. But what does He mean by that?

These verses are often interpreted with a focus on salvation; however, I think He means much more than the single choice of believing in Him as your Lord and Savior. Remember, your eternal life is a story of a journey, not a single choice. You are walking a path toward the Kingdom dwelling as you live your life. The farther you walk along the path during your lifetime, the closer you are to your dwelling place when you reach heaven.

Jesus never intended for you to be on your own. He wasn't telling Thomas, "It's up to you to figure it out." *Self-sufficiency is the way of the wide road.* I believe Jesus is saying you'll only make it to the dwelling place of the Father if your journey is a story of partnership, and you walk the narrow path *with Him*—not in the sense of believing He's "up there" watching over you, but in the very real sense of Jesus being your Guide, walking side by side with you, leading you in each step you make, speaking to your heart with encouragement and instruction, taking your hand to help you take the leap into the Kingdom life.

Born Naked

In response to news of great loss and suffering, Job "fell to the ground in worship and said: 'Naked I came from my mother's womb, and naked I will depart. The LORD gave and the LORD has taken away; may the name of the LORD be praised'" (Job 1:20-21). Ecclesiastes also states, "Everyone comes naked from their mother's womb, and as everyone comes, so they depart" (5:15).

Similarly, of Adam and Eve it is said, "Adam and his wife were both naked, and they felt no shame" (Genesis 2:25). And what was the first thing they realized after they chose to believe the serpent's deception over God's instruction and ate of the fruit of knowledge of good and evil? "Then the eyes of both of them were opened, and they realized they were naked; so they sewed fig leaves together and made coverings for themselves" (Genesis 3:7). Covering themselves—the universal response of shame.

Like Adam, we are all born naked, with nothing but our identities—our God-given natures, including whatever aspects of God's Spirit He created to be part of who we are—within us. And like Adam, others—whether it's parents, caregivers, teachers, authority figures, friends, society, the culture, or the enemy—begin to immediately tempt us to change in some way—to alter or add to or subtract from in order to *cover up* that nature.

God says He blesses you "in all things at all times, having all that you need" (II Corinthians 9:8). In other words, you have all you need in life from the start, and all you have is *your identity* and *His presence.* Your identity is all you bring to the table, both in this life and to the next.

How important, then, is it to live according to your true nature?

If that's all you have and all you need—and it is enough—it's vital you don't allow others to steal it from you, and you don't cover it up from fear or shame because you believe it isn't good enough. The more you strive to be good enough, the more you recognize your flaws and failings until you're left feeling you will never be good enough to receive the love of God. Perfectionism is the enemy of self-valuing.

It's important for you to value your true identity as God values you. Your identity is the one thing you have in this life that is completely yours—a gift from God, freely given, to be treasured for its glory and beauty and worth. The world may never see it for what it is, but not because it's any less wonderful or valuable—it is, in fact, one-of-a-kind and priceless—but because the world doesn't have eyes to see.

Imagine how you would see the world if you were always looking through a pair of green-tinted sunglasses. Everything would look green, right? The sky, the clouds, the river, the face of your friend, the walls of your home, even your own arms and legs would appear greenish. Your perception would alter your understanding of reality.

The world doesn't have spiritual eyes to see God's reality. Those bound to the world have "sunglasses" tinted according to the worldly view. If *self* were a color, it would be the hue of their lenses. They see how things affect them and choose their values and actions accordingly. They judge on surface appearances colored by their lenses but don't see past the exterior to the heart or the spirit of the individual. They judge themselves and project those judgments onto others. They cling to the world while rejecting God, including everything and everyone exuding His presence. Such people are described in II Timothy 3:2&4 as "lovers of themselves...(and) lovers of pleasure rather than lovers of God."

The world abhors the presence of God. As James 4:4 states, "friendship with the world means enmity against God." If God is in you, then the world will hate you as well, as Jesus said in John 15:19— "If you belonged to the world, it would love you as its own. As it is, you do not belong to the world, but I have chosen you out of the world. That is why the world hates you." When praying for His disciples, Jesus said, "the world has hated them, for they are not of the world, any more than I am of the world" (John 17:14).

Do you see why the world and all who are bound to it push you to reject your true nature and cover up your God-given identity?

Consider all the ways you've been told, in some form or fashion, that you're not good enough. Measurements begin almost immediately. You are weighed, compared, graded, critiqued, and judged by the worldly system, which is a system built to find flaw. In effect, no one can measure up. Yet, God calls His creation, "Good." The dichotomy between the world and the Kingdom is never more evident than in this example. How can you be created "in His own image" (Genesis 1:27), with aspects of God's own nature within you, and at the same time not be good enough? Do you see why you cannot live in the Kingdom and in the world simultaneously?

In addition to your story being about your journey to the dwelling Jesus prepared for you, yours is a story about the redemptive process to reclaim your true identity. Living from your God-given identity is necessary to live fully in the dwelling place of the Father. The naked fullness of who He created you to be, made whole again by the work of His hands, cleansed and purified by His death on the cross, is who He welcomes into His dwelling place.

Walking the Neural Pathways

I mentioned earlier the immediate, concerted efforts made by the world and the evil one to cover up your nature. As a child, you internalize those beliefs, words, and experiences until you have well-worn pathways within yourself, paths which Jesus must recreate to set your feet on His Kingdom road. But these paths are not external ones. They are pathways inside your brain.

Let's say you're the youngest in your family, close enough in age to your older siblings to believe you can do whatever they can do but young enough to fall short each time you try. Perhaps your parents and siblings find it humorous as you attempt to keep up with your siblings as they run across the yard. Or perhaps, your parents overtly compare you to your siblings and ask why you aren't able to do it like they can, or your siblings make fun of you for being slower. Either way, you may interpret these responses as meaning you are not good enough or you don't measure up.

That belief is a seed burrowing into your neural pathways in the deepest part of your brain. As the seed is watered (for example, at school when you make a poor grade on a test or from a peer who rejects your friendship), it grows and chokes out the good plants around it and spreads its roots far and wide. You walk this pathway quite often—at first, whenever circumstances water and fertilize the weeds, but soon you walk it constantly because you begin to interpret everything through the lens of that belief. Every little mistake becomes proof-text of your assertion that you will never measure up. And the enemy is quick to whisper his agreement with your interpretation and point out more proof-text from your experiences.

Over time, this process creates a well-developed neural pathway that operates very much like a dirt road with a groove in it from being well-traveled. Your feet get stuck in the groove, so you stay on the road, going over and over the same ground. Your belief feels so true to you, you feel unable to jolt yourself out of the rut. So, you walk the same road again and again, sealing your belief and grinding yourself deeper into the hole you've created.

Until Jesus comes in with a radical idea— "Let's travel on another path. A *new path*. One of my creation, made from my truth." He sets out to pull up the tendrils of weeds from the deep places and sow the truth about your identity (which somewhere even deeper than the far-reaching roots of the weeds, you've known from your naked birth), thus beginning to establish His new neural pathway. Now, there's a good bit of clearing to do, but He is a determined, persevering farmer with tons of experience planting seeds.

The problem is, He needs your cooperation. As a free being, created with the ability to choose, you are a partner with Him in the sowing process. You have the authority to aid in the process or to undo Jesus' work. Unfortunately, the old neural pathway with its "not enough" belief is familiar and oft used, and the enemy is well-aware of this fact. He seeks to exploit it at every turn. Before Jesus' new seeds are fully developed, the evil one will highlight a mistake and accuse you with a sneering, "See, I told you so" to entice you to retread old ground. If you indulge him and agree to walk the old pathway, your choice can damage the new seedlings and grind them back into the dirt, forcing Jesus to start over again. And each time you reinforce the old pathway, you make the belief feel more true, familiar, and enticing.

The good news is you also have the ability to choose to walk Jesus' new neural pathway. The more you reinforce His truth with *acceptance, trust,* and *action* (the definition of *faith*), the stronger His pathway becomes and the more the truth seeds stretch their roots through the soil of your heart.

Acceptance takes the form of believing what Jesus has told you and believing His teaching in Scripture. Of course, the lie belief "feels" true—you've walked that ground for a long time. You've collected tons of evidence of its validity along the way because you've been using the lenses of the belief itself to perceive and interpret your circumstances. But it doesn't matter how it feels—it only matters how it is. Jesus asks for radical acceptance. That's the nature of the Kingdom.

Trust goes even deeper than acceptance. Trust includes reliance on His truth, like an infant relies on his mother to feed him, or a small child jumping into a pool relies on her parent to catch her and hold her head above water, or a grown man relies on the floor to be there to meet his feet when he gets out of bed in the morning.

Consider how many things you rely on without question. (A clear example from recent events during the COVID pandemic is our reliance on the store having toilet paper or the gas station having gas when we need it—look at the strange behavior, even panic, that ensued when our trust proved invalid.) You flip a switch assuming the light will turn on. You open your computer assuming the internet will be there to transmit your email. I could keep going, but I think you get the point. Yet, when it comes to Jesus, radical acceptance and absolute reliance seem more difficult.

You might explain you have experience with toilet paper being in the store and gas being at the pump, and that's why you rely on those things. I'd point back to Ecclesiastes and remind you the things of this world are transient vapors, as our collective experience recently demonstrated. I'd also suggest if you paid closer attention, without assuming you are in control or determine your own outcomes, you would see evidence of God's hand at work in every aspect of your life. It's just that most people don't pay attention and tend to credit themselves when things work out well or they manage to make it through difficulty.

But the deepest form of trust is developed through relationship. My reliance on Jesus is based on His long-standing, connected presence—His guiding hand when I ask which way to go, His words of warning when I need to turn another direction, His word pictures when I need to understand a concept, His loving kindness when I mess things up, and His own radical acceptance of who I am. Our relationship has been built through years of intimate communication and effort from both sides, just like a good marriage.

The final element of faith is taking action based on your acceptance and trust, allowing His new neural pathway to guide your steps. James 2:17 says, "faith by itself, if it is not accompanied by action, is dead." Stated differently, acceptance and trust have no meaning or power if they don't produce any fruit in you. As Isaiah 55:10-11 describes it, "As the rain and the snow come down from heaven, and do not return to it without watering the earth and making it bud and flourish, so that it yields seed for the sower and bread for the eater, so is my word that goes out from my mouth." When you receive truth from Jesus in the deep places, it produces *change*.

In my example of believing you're not good enough, action could take the form of treating yourself with respect. It could look like allowing your inner nature to flow freely into the world. It could be doing something for yourself you've always wanted to do but never felt worthy to receive. It could take the form of setting boundaries in a relationship that has taken advantage of your belief you didn't measure up and acted as a reinforcer for the old pathway. It could mean standing up for your rights at work or refusing to be verbally demeaned at home. It could look like seeking to make new friends at church, with your heart believing you are someone others would want to have as a friend.

I have given one example of a lie belief embedded in a neural pathway, but we have an estimated hundred *trillion* neural connections in our brain, and who knows how many lie beliefs wander along those neural pathways. Do you see why I emphasize we can't walk the narrow path without Jesus?

But God always manages to take the impossible and simplify it. At the base of all lie beliefs is that nasty root of sin in Eden that *I can be like God*—the lie none of us want to relinquish. If you allow Jesus to cut this tap root, the whole lie-based system dies on the vine. Your role here is willingness, because you aren't able to reach that deeply entrenched root, much less cut it. Its substance is what Paul calls the flesh (or sin nature): "Those who live according to the flesh have their minds set on what the flesh desires; but those who live in accordance with the Spirit have their minds set on what the Spirit desires. The mind governed by the flesh is death, but the mind governed by the Spirit is life and peace" (Romans 8:5-6).

Basically, your lies are like a house of cards or a Jenga tower—remove the right card or block, and the structure tumbles. The sin nature—the belief I can be my own God—is the critical block connecting and holding up the entire structure of old neural pathways.

When your true, God-given identity is revealed to you, and you, in faith, radically accept, trust, and act from your true identity, the systemic lies that have oppressed your identity fall, and you and Jesus begin your journey on the new neural pathways. Along the way, He plants seeds of truth of all kinds, to prevent a reintroduction of the old neural pathways and to keep your feet on His desired path. The journey toward the fulfillment of your identity is a growth process made up of Jesus' plantings and your choices to walk where He walks.

What Matters?

So far, I've been focused on your journey on the Kingdom path toward your dwelling place in the Father's house, but why does this journey matter? Isn't it enough to simply accept Jesus as Savior and live life in expectation of the promised heaven?

Not according to Jesus.

The story of the wealthy man who asked what *good thing* he must *do* to get eternal life is one example of Jesus' call to the journey. Jesus' response is interesting. Initially, He challenged the man on his question. "Why do you ask me about what is good?...There is only One who is good" (Matthew 19:17). Essentially, Jesus is challenging the man's root lie, saying, "Only God is good, and you aren't God. You aren't able to be truly good."

We have aspects of God's nature that He has knit within us, but we are not God. We are good enough for God's love, but we are not good. We are not worthy of salvation, but we are worth saving.

You can't earn God's love or deserve His sacrifice; He gives them to you freely.

Jesus goes on to add, "If you want to enter life, keep the commandments." Notice He didn't say "if you want to enter *eternal* life." Jesus is reminding the man here of one reason the commandments were given—to benefit Israel so God's children could have a rich, fulfilled life.

The wealthy man presses Jesus further, so He lists some of the commandments, which the man claims to have kept. Then, in an unexpected twist, Jesus responds, "If you want to be perfect, go, sell your possessions and give to the poor, and you will have treasure in heaven. Then come, follow me" (v. 21). As you know, the wealthy man chose instead to walk away.

Jesus, in that moment, was more interested in addressing the two greatest obstacles to wholeness, fulfillment, and joy in the wealthy man's life. The first obstacle was his belief he could somehow be like God, and his effort at goodness would buy him a ticket to eternal life. Quite the opposite, as Jesus stated. The man missed the point of all of it—life, the Kingdom, the commandments—because he remained bound to the flesh (or sin nature) and was still trying to be his own God and walk the path alone. His view of God was through a lens of exchange—I get this in exchange for that—a relational economy instead of a love relationship.

The second obstacle was the man's valuing of his wealth over his own heart. Rather than pouring into life and others out of his abundance, he hoarded riches as if his wealth had intrinsic value. Perhaps he believed his wealth afforded him power or position, or perhaps he was invested in the security he thought his wealth provided. More likely, the young man equated his wealth with his identity, and to give it away would mean losing the one thing that made him feel valuable and valued. Whatever his justification, his wealth held more value to him even than the state of his eternal soul or his God-given identity. The man wanted the ultimate reward, but he didn't want the relationship or the journey. He didn't know what his true treasure was—the treasure that would bring the Kingdom into his life.

When Jesus told the disciples, "it is easier for a camel to go through the eye of a needle than for someone who is rich to enter the Kingdom of God" (v. 24), He is teaching them the impossibility of overcoming our worldly, fleshly beliefs without God's help, and the devastation caused by valuing worldly things over matters of the heart, such as relationship and restoration. In this story, Jesus is showing the disciples how much the journey of your life matters.

He is also bringing an added element—that pouring out from your true heart into others is a key part of the journey. Living from your true identity means allowing your nature to flow freely into the world. In much the same way Jesus instructed the wealthy man not to hoard his riches but to sell it and give to the poor, you are not to hoard your true nature in your heart, held captive or in hiding, away from others. The expression of your identity is to be lived out, not held in—given freely to others, not kept to yourself.

Through this story, Jesus is also showing how much every choice matters. The wealthy man wasn't a bad man, not by any human measure. He reportedly kept the commandments. He even sought answers to try to be better. Choice after choice set his feet on the narrow path to the Kingdom. Yet, the two obstacles remained, and when it came time to choose the ultimate surrender of the things he valued most, his choice was to walk away. And yes, according to Jesus, that one choice placed the man's feet on the wide path toward destruction.

The man isn't without hope, however, for when asked, given the insurmountable obstacles, who can be saved, Jesus said, "With man this is impossible, but with God all things are possible" (v. 26). Once again, Jesus emphasizes you aren't making this journey on your own—you can't, and you aren't intended to. Remember, Jesus' instruction to the wealthy man ended with, "come, follow me."

So, how you live your life matters, and the choices you make have eternal consequences. Your willingness to surrender the flesh (or sin nature) to Jesus for its destruction matters. "For when we were in the realm of the flesh, the sinful passions aroused by the law were at work in us, so that we bore fruit for death...Those who are in the realm of the flesh cannot please God...For if you live according to the flesh, you will die; but if by the Spirit you put to death the misdeeds of the body, you will live" (Romans 7:5, 8:8, 13).

What does it mean to truly surrender? According to Romans 10:3, Hebrews 12:9, James 4:7, and other, similar verses, to surrender means to submit to God and His righteousness.

Before I go further, I want to unpack the word, submit. In English, submit is a hierarchical term meaning to yield to a superior force or person; however, the word translated "submit" in the New Testament, *hupotasso,* has a different connotation. It is a military term referring to *aligning* in correct order by locking shields with fellow warriors on the battlefield—not coming under but coming alongside—without hierarchy. This is a crucial distinction, because coming under can be misinterpreted as giving control to someone, and control is not what Jesus wants. *Letting go* of the illusion of control and self-determination is what He desires for you. To submit is to come into true partnership—moving together as one.

To walk the narrow paths, you must come alongside Jesus and partner with Him on the journey. As I've stated, you can't rip out the root lie of the sin nature that exists in all of us on your own. You need His help. Walking in alignment with Him and making your choices together with Him—not giving up your choice but sharing in it with Him—will, by definition, keep your feet on the narrow way.

Jesus has already walked the narrow path. He knows the way.

In the story of your journey to the Father's dwelling place, your identity also matters. Like any artist, God looks upon you, the work of His hands, and sees a masterpiece (Ephesians 2:10). He loves His creation, and He created you on purpose. He was intentional in the elements of His nature He chose to knit together in you (Psalm 139:13). Out of that reflection of His nature, your identity was created to flow into the world, with the goal of helping Him bring restoration and usher in the return of His Kingdom. He's given you a magnificent purpose.

It stands to reason, then, that if your true identity matters, what you pour into others and into the world matters. Just like the nature of the main character is crucial to a good book or movie, you are crucial in God's Kingdom. Of course, without the main character, there is no story. But beyond that, the qualities of the character, in large part, determine the quality of the story.

Every Christmas Eve, my husband and I watch the movie, *It's a Wonderful Life*, as part of our Christmas traditions. Talk about a story with great characters! My favorite line is spoken by an angel: "Each man's life touches so many other lives. When he isn't around, he leaves an awful hole, doesn't he?"

If you cover up or hide away your true identity, the reason for your being is thwarted. Just like George Bailey, you leave an awful hole—a hole no one else can fill. Just think how different George's town became when he was missing (if you haven't seen the movie, what was once a lovely, quaint community becomes a seedy, lewd, and bitter town controlled by an evil man).

If you are missing in action, the coming of God's Kingdom is altered. All the lives you could've touched along the narrow paths are changed by your absence. Yes, one person makes a big difference. The evil one likes to whisper that we don't matter, that our absence would make no difference. Remember in those moments, everything out of the enemy's mouth is a lie (John 8:44).

The question is not if you have an impact. You do. The question is, what kind of impact do you want to have? Are you furthering the Kingdom on earth or hindering it? When you live according to your true identity and pour into others from your true heart, you further the Kingdom.

Finally, what you value matters. Are things of this world of more worth to you than your relationship with Jesus? Your true identity? Your journey to the Kingdom?

If you spend more of your time, energy, effort, and focus on building up your sense of control, power, security, safety, self-protection, self-gratification, self-sufficiency, self-determination, acceptability in the world's eyes, and avoidance of pain and suffering than you do on deepening your relationship with Jesus, accepting His truth, building your trust and reliance on Him, and reclaiming and living out of your true identity, your values still bind you to the wide path.

At this point, you might argue you have to focus on the worldly in order to survive. You likely have a job, which takes up a huge chunk of time and energy. You may have children or family who also eat up time and energy. You have chores to do, meals to prepare, bills to pay—I know. So do I. But in asking this question, you're assuming it is an either/or. In other words, either I'm focusing on my responsibilities, or I'm focusing on Jesus.

What if, instead, you partner *with* Jesus in your responsibilities? What if you share your day-to-day experiences with Him? In fact, if He lives within you, aren't you doing that already? All that's missing is a shift in your *focus.* "So we fix our eyes not on what is seen, but on what is unseen, since what is seen is temporary, but what is unseen is eternal" (II Corinthians 4:18).

When you become *aware* of His presence with you at all times and in all things, it's a game-changer. Not only will your burden lighten, and your attitude become more positive, you'll have an ever-present Guide in your choice-making, increasing the likelihood your steps will remain planted on the narrow paths. It isn't an either/or. It's a yes-and. As the writer of Hebrews describes it, "let us run with perseverance the race marked out for us, fixing our eyes on Jesus, the pioneer and perfecter of faith" (Hebrews 12:1-2). You can run the race with perseverance *and* fix your eyes on Jesus.

In truth, the only reason you *can* run the race—the journey to your dwelling place—with perseverance is *because* you have your eyes fixed on the One who establishes and perfects your faith. Of everything that matters in your story, journeying with Jesus is the one thing that matters above all else.

Consider This

1. What feelings and thoughts arise in you as you read this sentence? *Each and every choice, from the largest to the most seemingly insignificant, affects your experience of the story.*

2. The story of your journey has twists and turns along the way. How would you describe your life journey so far?

3. Imagine your dwelling place with Jesus. What images come to mind for you? What would you desire? What are your hopes?

4. I describe three dimensions of your journey to your Kingdom dwelling place: the journey to the deep places within your heart, the journey toward heaven, and the continuous journey of choices between divergent paths. Considering each dimension, think about how you are faring. In what ways have you tried to walk the journey alone? Where do you need to include Jesus as your partner on the journey?

5. In what ways are you like the children of Israel as described in Psalm 107? In what ways has God responded to your cries and brought you out?

6. Ecclesiastes talks about the things of the world as *hebel*—transient and fleeting. Where in your life have you experienced the *hebel* nature of worldly values?

7. In what ways have you tried to live with one foot in the world and one in the Kingdom? What are the places in your life where you've stepped fully with both feet into the Kingdom ways?

8. I use the analogy of tinted lenses to talk about how our beliefs color our perceptions. Think about the color of your lenses. Do you tend to take a dark or bright view of yourself? Of others? What beliefs color your lenses?

9. What feelings and thoughts arise when you read this statement? *You have all you need in life from the start, and all you have is your identity and His presence. Your identity is all you bring to the table, both in this life and to the next.*

10. Think about your earliest experiences. What neural pathways do you believe were laid in as seeds in your brain early in your life? How have those seeds been watered and nurtured throughout your life?

11. I define faith as acceptance, trust, and action. What are your thoughts on my definition of faith?

12. Look at the things you focus on the majority of the time. Think about what kinds of things get the strongest emotional responses from you and what kinds of things spur you to action. Try to be honest with yourself as you make a list of these things. These are your values. What did you discover?

13. What are the obstacles in your life to wholeness, fulfillment, and joy? Where have you found wholeness, fulfillment, and joy in your life? Do you see the hand of Jesus in those places?

14. Have you thought of submission as coming under God's control? What are your thoughts and feelings about the definition of

surrender as aligning yourself with Jesus in partnership, like a warrior locking shields with a fellow warrior?

15. What thoughts and feelings arise when you hear Clarence's quote from *It's a Wonderful Life?* *"Each man's life touches so many other lives. When he isn't around, he leaves an awful hole, doesn't he?"*

CHAPTER TWO
PROMISED LAND, PROMISED DWELLING

In Chapter One, we took a look at the description of the Israelites' choices in Psalm 107 as an example of walking the wide paths toward destruction. Let's revisit their story to see what else it has to teach us about our path to the promised dwelling place with the Father.

When Moses stood before the burning bush on Mount Horeb, God spoke to him of bringing His people out of the land of Egypt. "I have indeed seen the misery of my people in Egypt. I have heard them crying out because of their slave drivers, and I am concerned about their suffering. So I have come down to rescue them from the hand of the Egyptians and to bring them up out of that land into a good and spacious land, a land flowing with milk and honey—the home of the Canaanites, Hittites, Amorites, Perizzites, Hivites and Jebusites. And now the cry of the Israelites has reached me, and I have seen the way the Egyptians are oppressing them. So now, go. I am sending you to Pharaoh to bring my people the Israelites out of Egypt" (Exodus 3:7-10).

Once again, the story speaks of God hearing their cries and coming to rescue them from their distress to take them to a new land—a new dwelling place. What were the responses to God's coming?

The first response was from Moses, who went straight for self-negation. "Who am I to do this thing You're asking?" (v. 11). Does this sound familiar to you? Remember the self lies from the previous chapter ("I'm not worthy, I'm not good enough, I don't matter")? God's reply is familiar, too: "I will be with you" (v. 12). These elements, consistent with our own experiences, show up in this interaction with God: God's promise of a new dwelling place, self lies in response to

God's call to the journey, and God's further promise to come along with us on the journey.

Moses' next response was a 'what if' (4:1), a fear-based response questioning the power of God's presence, to which God responded with power. Then, Moses questioned the effectiveness of his identity for the journey ("I have never been eloquent...I am slow of speech and tongue" v. 10), and God pointed out, as the one who created Moses, He knew what Moses was capable of, and He offered to help Moses know what to say (v. 11-12). Moses' final position was avoidance, begging God to send someone else on the difficult journey (v. 13) but God would have none of it, and finally, off Moses went.

We also reply with "what if's" to God's call to walk the narrow paths. "What if something bad happens? What if I get hurt because I've put down my guard? What if it's too hard or too painful? What if I fail?" These are just some of the questions we might throw out in response to God. At the root, "what if's" come down to the fear that God is not enough. By extension, we also fear that we are not enough.

We doubt our equipping by God for the journey. Like Moses, we question if our identity will be enough to get the job done. We don't trust God knows what He's doing, and come back with, "Surely, not me, Lord!" instead of, "Yes, Lord, send me."

If there's any way to get out of hardship, we are likely to try any means at our disposal to avoid it. We see pain as a negative, a threat to us. The humanness of Jesus in the Garden of Gethsemane can be seen as He, too, begs God to take the cup from Him. The difference is, He doesn't stop there. He continues His conversation with God, saying, "Yet, not as I will, but as you will" (Matthew 26:39). He saw the pain and suffering in light of the great good coming from it.

At first, the Israelites believed that God had seen their misery and heard their cries for help, and they bowed down and worshipped Him (v. 31). But when things got hard, the grumbling and blaming started. "Make the work harder for the people," Pharoah commanded

(5:9), and the people became bitter toward Moses and accused him (v. 21), and he in turn accused God (v. 23).

God's reply was to remind Moses of His identity ("I am the Lord"—6:2) and to reiterate His promises of deliverance to a new dwelling, but the Israelites "did not listen to him because of their discouragement and harsh labor" (v. 9), and Moses offers one more proof text of his incapability, saying why would Pharoah listen "since I speak with faltering lips" (v. 30).

You can see the additional elements of fear and shame/blame showing up in these interactions with God, as well as bitterness, doubting God's character, and accusation against God. All these hindrances to the journey to the new dwelling place are consistent with our responses when faced with hardship along the journey. When things get rough, we tend to turn our anger toward God, blaming Him instead of placing responsibility on the enemy, the sin choices of others, or our own sin choices for our difficulties. We also succumb readily to fear, which leads to self-doubt and self-debasement. We close our ears to God's voice in our fear and shame/blame and bitterness, at the very time we need to hear Him most.

When Moses and Aaron started doing what the Lord told them to do, that's when things started happening. At the last plague on the firstborn, God changed their calendar to reflect their new beginning (12:2) and instituted a sign—the Passover (v. 3-14)—to point toward the ultimate sacrifice of the Lamb of God, our *new beginning* for our journey. He made it a "lasting ordinance" (v. 14), for it reflects the coming of Jesus, His sacrifice, and His bringing us out of death into the new, eternal dwelling with Him. What a beautiful picture of what was to come!

Still, even with the miracles of the Passover and the parting of the seas, the trust of the people was short-lived. As soon as they ran out of water, the grumbling began again (15:24). God provided their water but followed up with another instruction, for the people to listen carefully to Him and do what is right in His eyes instead of their own (v.

26). Sadly, they weren't able to pull this off, either. It wasn't long before they pined for the life they had before they started this new journey. "If only we had died by the LORD's hand in Egypt! There we sat around pots of meat and ate all the food we wanted, but you have brought us out into this desert to starve this entire assembly to death" (Exodus 16:3).

How many of us have received the outpouring of God's love with gratitude only to bemoan our fate a short while later? Like the Israelites, our memories are very brief before we become consumed with our current circumstances and forget all He has done for us.

You have to marvel at God's patience. Once again, He heard their complaint and provided manna for them to eat (v. 15). Even with the manna, they couldn't follow His simple instructions to eat only what was provided for them each day (v. 20).

At this point, lest you get caught up in judgment against the Israelites or think, "I would never do that," I want to remind you that we share these same responses to God along our journey. The Israelites are just like us. We listen to fear. We grumble and complain about our circumstances. We get angry at God when bad things happen. We don't listen to His guidance. We fall back into old patterns and old beliefs when things get hard. We run headlong (and headstrong) ahead of Him to try to determine the path of our lives. Rather than judge them critically, I pray we can learn from their mistakes.

Fast forward to the great sin of the Israelites of rejecting God and making a golden idol to worship (Exodus 32:1). God described it this way: "They have been quick to turn away from what I commanded them" (v. 8). Only Moses' pleading intervention on their behalf prevented their destruction.

We, too, make idols for ourselves to worship, idols made up of the "treasures" of the world. Our idols may not be calves of gold, but they are just as deadly to us—things like our desire for approval from others, for which we are willing to sacrifice our identities; like our desire for security and safety, at the cost of our God-given freedom; like our desire for power and control, flowing from the root Edenic sin of self as God; like our desire for success or status as defined by the world instead of as defined by Christ; like our desire for our base wants to be gratified, at the expense of our self-respect; like our demand for someone else to "make us" feel special, beautiful or handsome, and loved, even if we have to sell our souls to get it. Like the Israelites, we reject God's ways in favor of these false gods, and only God's intervention on our behalf saves us from ourselves.

Enter or Wander?

When the Israelites finally arrived at the Promised Land, the Lord instructed Moses to send one man from each tribe to investigate their new land (Numbers 13). Their report, while admitting the land was as God described, was quite frightening—fortified cities, powerful men, even Nephilim. The people reacted much as we do when we face difficulty and hardship: "If only we had died in Egypt! Or in this wilderness! Wouldn't it be better for us to go back to Egypt?" (14:2, 3).

Our version of dying in the wilderness or going back to Egypt is returning to captivity to the old ways and the wide paths. We cling to our lies like they're life preservers instead of heavy chains. We revert to the old, well-worn neural pathways and familiar behavior patterns, no matter how miserable we were the last time we lived there. We self-sabotage, undermining whatever gains Jesus has made along the narrow paths within us, stomping down His new seedlings of truth as we rush to get away from the perceived threat.

Only Joshua and Caleb resisted the fear, focusing instead on the presence of the Lord, saying, "The Lord is with us. Do not be afraid" (v. 9). And what did the Israelites do? They talked about stoning Joshua and Caleb for daring to accept God's promise, trust His instructions, and enter the land.

Ten times as they journeyed, the Israelites treated God with contempt, refused to believe Him, disobeyed His instructions, and tested Him (v. 11, 22). On the cusp of receiving the great and wonderful promise of God, a beautiful new land to call their own, their failure to complete the trust and action parts of faith left them outside the dwelling place, wandering in the wilderness until the entire generation who had tested God died—all except Caleb and Joshua, men of a "different spirit" (v. 24) who were willing to follow God through the whole journey. The wanderers received what they asked for—to perish in the wilderness.

God graciously allows us to choose. As part of our freedom, we are given the right to self-sabotage and self-destruct, if that is our choice. But what would motivate us to choose in such a way? Let's explore what left the Israelites wandering and see what we can learn about ourselves.

First, we know from God's description that the Israelites were "stiff-necked" (Exodus 32:9), meaning haughty, stubborn, antagonistic, arrogant, demanding, and argumentative. Do you recognize the lie belief behind all of these traits? Yes, we are back to the root lie of Eden—self as God. Basically, they thought they knew better. They wanted things their way. They lived by the creed: *we want what we want when we want it.* Envision Tolkien's Gollum: "We wants it. We needs it, precious."

They also misperceived God's love through the lens of a relational economy. God offered repeatedly to journey with them and freely give them a beautiful new dwelling place, but they wanted control more than they wanted relationship with God. Since they were incapable of genuine love (which means love offered freely as a gift rather than through exchange), they couldn't imagine God loving them in that way. Therefore, they kept the relationship on a surface level. Their internal language probably sounds something like this: *sure, we'll follow you, as long as—* (fill in the blank).

They couldn't see their own value in God's eyes. It's almost as if their consistent, unstated question was: *why would God do all this for us?* They never fully trusted God to provide for them and protect them on the journey, so when the hard times arose, they balked and complained and succumbed to fear. They had nothing relational to stand on, no assurance in God's tremendous love for them—despite all the evidence He had given them—perhaps due to their lack of self-worth. They accepted the things God did for them but failed to allow the truth to transform their hearts and produce fruit. As a result, they had the attitude: *what have you done for me lately?*

Their outlook was consistently negative, predicting the worst in every scenario. This response is a form of self-protection and is rooted in fear. The belief is: *I can protect myself if I anticipate the worst possible outcomes because then I won't be surprised or disappointed.* Sadly, through anticipating the worst, their choices often produced the very thing they feared. Also, they lost the joy of the amazing experience of following God's cloud and fire, and the wonder of being with His presence in the Tent of Meeting, because their negative outlook robbed them of the joy. They were so preoccupied with their belief in the bad thing happening, they lost sight of all else.

Like we discussed in Chapter One, they desired an easy road. They weren't willing to face the difficult parts of the journey by walking through them with God. They thought His presence wasn't enough, so they rationalized fleeing back to how it used to be rather than risking the unknown of the new path. They told themselves: *this is hard; surely it would be better to go back.* They wanted the familiar. They desired safety and ease.

Of course, Egypt might've been familiar, but it certainly wasn't safe or easy for them. But distance distorted their memory of their captivity, making it appear better than the hardship in their current circumstance, and their rationalizations made them comfortable with their memory distortions. As a result, they didn't commit God's interventions on their behalf to long-term memory. They focused on the immediate struggle and took their eyes off God. Distraction caused them to forget all He had already done and center only on what was happening in their circumstances.

Now, let's go back and substitute your story for the story of Israel. Have you ever approached God with your demands or argued with Him about what He wanted to do? Have you ever been angry, bitter, or frustrated with God for not giving you what you wanted? Have you gone ahead of God and done things your way without checking in with Him to find out what He thought was best for you? Have you questioned God's motives and doubted His goodness and love toward you?

Have you ever felt like your relationship with God was a quid pro quo economy, where you believed He owed you or you owed Him? Have you found yourself forgetting God's truth He has told you in light of struggles in your present circumstances? Have you taken on the role of being your own protector by keeping a negative outlook, anticipating bad things to keep from being disappointed or asking yourself 'what if?' questions to try to guard yourself against bad things happening to you?

Have you ever fallen into the trap of going back to old beliefs and behaviors because things in your life got difficult? Have you fled from God because you didn't want to face hardship or struggle or deal with something unknown? Have you rationalized your choices through self-justification or blaming God or others? Have you ever chosen perceived safety over your relationship with God?

Each of these choices tramps on the old, familiar, wide pathways, reforging and reinforcing them, threatening to leave you as a wanderer in the wilderness once more.

If you said *yes* to several of these questions, don't feel bad. Anyone who is honest will answer *yes* to many of them. The sin nature is in all of us. Even the great apostle, Paul, said, "For I have the desire to do what is good, but I cannot carry it out. For I do not do the good I want to do, but the evil I do not want to do—this I keep on doing...Although I want to do good, evil is right there with me. For in my inner being I delight in God's law; but I see another law at work in me, waging war against the law of my mind and making me a prisoner of the law of sin at work within me. What a wretched man I am!" (Romans 7:18-19, 21-24).

What hope is there, then? If we are prisoner of the sin nature at work in us, are we doomed to wander in our own form of wilderness forever?

With great joy, I respond as Paul did when the Galatians got his teaching so wrong: Absolutely not! *We know Jesus!* Paul goes on the ask in verse 24, "Who will rescue me from this body that is subject to death?" His answer? "Thanks be to God, who delivers me through Jesus Christ our Lord!" (v. 25). Jesus, who has walked the narrow path and who willingly desires to take our journey with us, is the power to overcome the sin nature within us. He is our Deliverer and our Redeemer. He can get to the deepest places in our hearts and minds, the places we can't reach, and gently, lovingly pull out the flesh/sin nature root buried within us.

Just as Moses, the promised deliverer, is the precursor to our final redemption purchased with the blood of Jesus and Passover points toward the once-and-for-all sacrifice of Jesus, Israel's Promised Land is a precursor, a mirror in which you can see the beautiful promise of God to deliver you from the clutches of evil, part whatever waters stand in your way, carry you across the wilderness in the covering of His cloud and the Holy Spirit's fire, and usher you into your Kingdom dwelling, victorious. And just as Jesus is superior to Moses (Hebrews 3:3-6) and the covenant sealed at the Last Supper is superior to the Passover (Matthew 26:28, Hebrews 8:6)), our Promised Dwelling Place is far superior to the Promised Land.

Kings and Altars and Foreign Gods

If ever a people deserved to be discarded, surely it was Israel. Yet, God didn't ever give up on them. After the forty years of wilderness walking, He made them triumphant in the land of promise and delivered the land into their hands. If only the story ended there...

God permitted the people of Israel once again to cleanse themselves from their sin and reengage the enemy who had defeated them. This time, they won the battle. Joshua then had all of the people renew their covenant with God (Joshua 8:30-35). Joshua waged war across the region until he had taken all the lands promised to Israel by God. Then, Israel lived in peace the remainder of Joshua's lifetime. Before he died, Joshua had the people once more renew their covenant with God. He also issued a warning: "If you forsake the LORD and serve foreign gods, he will turn and bring disaster on you and make an end of you, after he has been good to you...throw away the foreign gods that are among you and yield your hearts to the LORD, the God of Israel" (Joshua 24:20, 23).

But after Joshua's death, the next generation "knew neither the LORD nor what he had done for Israel. Then the Israelites did evil in the eyes of the LORD and served the Baals. They forsook the LORD, the God of their ancestors, who had brought them out of Egypt. They followed and worshiped various gods of the peoples around them" (Judges 2:10-12).

This begins a carousel of leaders, judges who would straighten things out temporarily, but when they died, the people went back to rebellion against God. Predictably, war and chaos ensued. Then, the people demanded a king, to be like other nations around them (I Samuel 8:5). Samuel, upset by their request, prayed, and God responded, "it is not you they have rejected, but they have rejected me as their king. As they have done from the day I brought them up out of Egypt until this day, forsaking me and serving other gods" (v. 7-8).

Although they rejected God as their King, He still loved them and cared for them. He had Samuel warn them of the consequences of having a king, but they wouldn't listen and continued to demand a king. Of course, the consequences came upon them, just as God described.

Another carousel begins, good kings followed by bad. For example, David, a good king whose heart was for God, was followed by Solomon, who had foreign wives (700 wives and 300 concubines—I Kings 11:3) and participated heavily in the worship of foreign gods. The bad kings outweighed the good, and eventually, the people had forgotten God, the Law, and everything God had done for them and were taken into captivity and the Temple destroyed.

Rather than remain set apart for God, the Israelites adopted the ways of the people they conquered. They married foreign women and built altars to worship foreign gods, even within the walls of the Temple. How easily and quickly, and how often, the children of Israel turned away from God, the One who saved them from Egypt. He gave them chance after chance, and restored them time and time again, only to have them once more turn their backs.

Like the people of Israel, you live in a foreign land, surrounded by people who worship foreign gods. But Jesus said you are not of this world (John 15:19, 17:14-16). You are a foreigner (I Peter 1:17, 2:11) in the literal sense of the word—the ways of the world are to be foreign to you. According to Paul, if you belong to Christ and are of the Kingdom, you "have crucified the flesh with its passions and desires" (Galatians 5:24). You've removed all altars to foreign gods and idols in your "Temple" (your heart). You no longer desire to live according to the flesh, as this world does. Your citizenship is elsewhere.

Empty Promises vs. Kingdom Living

As citizens of the Kingdom, we take the measure of all things by the fruit produced (Matthew 7:16). If something creates division, hostility, bitterness, hatred, malice, despair, emptiness, or hopelessness, we recognize these are not the fruits of the Spirit (Galatians 5:22-23). So, we know whatever produces these things is not of the Kingdom.

Worldly values often promise one thing but produce another. A simple example is the worldly urging to buy more, possess more, and chase more as a source of happiness, but the promise is empty or at best transient (remember our discussion on *hebel* in Ecclesiastes?) Because we are constantly inundated with advertisements touting the promise of "more," Kingdom living takes care we don't become worshippers of things.

Some other examples of worldly values which don't live up to their promises are seeking status or power or fame or wealth as a way to happiness, desiring security and safety as a way to find peace, and fleshly gratification as a way to find joy. None of these produce the desired results, finding emptiness, loneliness, insecurity, anxiety, and long-term unintended consequences instead.

Of course, the worldly perspective tends to seek instant gratification over long-term betterment, claiming immediate satisfaction is worth the long-term cost or not counting the cost at the outset. The world also tends to allow emotions to lead their choices instead of wisdom and truth, insisting their emotions are "valid" even if they are based on lie beliefs. Seeing the fruit of these beliefs, Kingdom living rejects them and holds to God's truth that genuine joy and peace are found within, through the presence of His Spirit in relationship, and not through external circumstances.

The enemy also likes to take positive values and distort them just enough to turn them in opposition to the Kingdom. An example of such a value is society's focus on saving the environment, a worthy and noble cause—as God's people we are called to care for and cherish His creation—and while we want to care for nature, Kingdom living doesn't go so far as to worship the created instead of its Creator.

God is a God of justice, so certainly justice is a Kingdom value. However, Kingdom living recognizes and maintains the distinction between justice and fairness. Justice has to do with the righteousness of God discriminating between right and wrong (e.g., it is wrong to take something that belongs to someone else), while fairness has to do with human beings attempting to produce a level playing field (it isn't fair that Suzy has a doll, and I don't). While we speak out for justice wherever we can, we don't expect fairness in this world. Fairness is impossible to achieve and isn't a Kingdom goal, whereas justice is.

Another positive belief growing in popularity in our culture is a desire to right wrongs from the past, but Kingdom living doesn't turn this goal into the acceptance of a victim mentality. While Jesus by worldly standards could've been viewed as a victim, given He was beaten and crucified, yet had done no wrong, He never saw Himself or acted like a victim. When He talked about giving up His life, He said, "No one takes it from me, but I lay it down of my own accord" (John 10:18) and "You would have no power over me if it were not given to you from above" (John 19:11). Following His example, Kingdom living seeks to right wrongs but rejects a victim mentality, teaching us to take personal responsibility for our actions, even when others don't.

Scripture tells us the importance of our freedom: "It is for freedom that Christ has set us free" (Galatians 5:1). Therefore, Kingdom living protects and defends freedom in all and for all. However, as Paul states, "do not use your freedom to indulge the flesh, rather, serve one another humbly in love" (Galatians 5:13). If we take advantage of our freedom to sin or cause harm to ourselves or others, we are opposing God's Kingdom. Again, Paul explains, "'Everything is lawful,' but not everything is beneficial. 'Everything is lawful,' but not everything builds others up" (I Corinthians 10:23 NET).

Above all, Kingdom living defends the truth—God's truth—and speaks the truth *in love* (Ephesians 4:15). But using the truth as a weapon against others is a distortion of God's intention. The truth is indeed a weapon, but it isn't to be used against people. It is given as armor, to "stand against the devil's schemes" (Ephesians 6:11). Truth is described as the belt (v. 14), which serves the function of holding the rest of our armor securely in place and strengthening our core to stand firm. A belt turned against others as a whip only promotes the devil's schemes.

We also reject extremes, remembering that temperance or balance is listed as a fruit of the Spirit (Galatians 5:23). Taking a stand for truth is certainly a Kingdom value, but we guard against becoming black-and-white thinkers and avoid either/or, legalistic mindsets where disagreement equals hatred, and the baby goes out with the bathwater. The Pharisees, for example, dealt in extremes—no work on the Sabbath meant you can't heal someone on the Sabbath (Luke 13:10-17), even though healing is an act of love and kindness, both fruits of the Spirit.

In the same way, Kingdom living avoids hypocrisy. Of all Jesus' criticisms of the Pharisees, He was most vehement about their hypocrisy, calling them "blind guides" and "whitewashed tombs" (Matthew 23:16, 27). He warned His disciples against what He called the "yeast" of the Pharisees and Sadducees (Matthew 16:6), referring to their hypocrisy. Instead, we allow the Kingdom of God to flow from within us into the world. But when we put ourselves forward as examples of righteousness and criticize or judge others, we become blind guides and whitewashed tombs like the Pharisees (remember Jesus' answer to the wealthy man— "There is only One who is good.") Instead, we adopt an attitude of humility, removing the log from our own eyes rather than plucking the speck from theirs (Matthew 7:1-3).

The journey to your Kingdom home within you produces responses in you which grow the fruits of the Spirit in abundance all around your dwelling. As you live your life in partnership with His Spirit, your dwelling place is enriched and made beautiful by His fruit, and that beauty can then flow freely from you to create change in the world and usher in God's Kingdom. Then, when you reach your dwelling place in heaven, your land will be overflowing with milk and honey, just like the Promised Land.

Belonging

So, if you are not of this world and are a foreigner here, where do you belong?

All human beings have an inherent desire to belong. God created us to be social creatures, connected and in relationship. After all, we are made in the image of God, and He exists in relationship (Father, Son, and Holy Spirit). *God created us for relationship.*

Even before birth, we begin the process of attachment and bonding. We already recognize our mother at birth. Babies come out groping for their mother. It's a built-in response. As soon as our eyes open and we make eye contact, we respond to stimuli and express the connection between caregiver and infant.

If we are made for relationship, and we're born connected and attached, how can we not belong?

Let's look back to Israel's example for our answers. First, they belonged to God—He made that truth crystal clear. When He made His covenant with Abraham, He stated, "I will establish my covenant as an everlasting covenant between me and you and your descendants after you for the generations to come, to be your God and the God of your descendants after you. The whole land of Canaan, where you now reside as a foreigner, I will give as an everlasting possession to you and your descendants after you; and I will be their God" (Genesis 17:7-8). This covenant began the series of events that ultimately led to Christ's coming, as God also promised Abraham that all nations would be blessed through him (Genesis 18:18), the promise of salvation coming through Abraham's descendant.

God repeated His promise to be the God of the Israelites and dwell with them in Exodus 29:45. Even after Israel rejected God, followed foreign gods, and were taken into captivity, God continued to affirm His promise: "I will give them a heart to know me, that I am the LORD. They will be my people, and I will be their God, for they will return to me with all their heart" (Jeremiah 24:7; see also, Jeremiah 31:33 and 32:38, and Ezekiel 11:20, 14:11, 34:24, 37:23, 37:27, and 39:28, and Zechariah 8:8).

Through Jesus Christ, God's promise is fulfilled. Our hearts are given to Him, and He dwells with us and within us. We are His people, and He is our God. We belong.

Israel also belonged in their land. It was their refusal to take the land where they belonged that left then as wanderers for forty years. In much the same way, we belong to the Kingdom, both the Kingdom within and the Kingdom in heaven. Our dwelling place is our land, and our home is with God.

Beyond these truths, the Israelites also belonged in the world. Now, they were indeed foreigners coming into the land before it was given to them by God, and afterwards, they lived among foreigners and were told not to adopt their ways or marry foreign wives, so they were not "of" the world. That didn't mean they didn't belong in it. God's promise that all nations would be blessed through Abraham's descendant meant His people not only belonged in the world, they were integral to the world's redemption.

Like the Israelites, we interact with the world as foreigners, but that doesn't mean we don't belong in the world. If we didn't, God would take us home. Like the descendants of Abraham, we have a crucial role to play in the world's restoration. We are called to usher in the Kingdom of God on earth, the coming of the new heaven and new earth described in Revelation 21. Our battle against the encroaching presence of the evil one reclaims land for the Kingdom toward Jesus' return, where all will be restored, and the problem of evil will be no more.

As Paul explains, "Consequently, you are no longer foreigners and strangers, but fellow citizens with God's people and also members of his household, built on the foundation of the apostles and prophets, with Christ Jesus himself as the chief cornerstone. In him the whole building is joined together and rises to become a holy temple in the Lord. And in him you too are being built together to become a dwelling in which God lives by his Spirit" (Ephesians 2:19-22). So, we are aliens to the world (not *of* it), *and* we belong *in* it, to partner with Jesus to complete the work He began when He brought the Kingdom of God to live within our hearts, building us to become His dwelling place until His Kingdom comes.

Parallels

I find the parallels between the stories of the Old Testament and the story of Jesus mind-blowing. What a wondrous and beautiful picture He gives us of His heart. The Old Testament is a story of God's faithfulness and relentless pursuit of His people. The coming of Christ is the ultimate act of pursuit, showing to what lengths He is willing to go to have relationship with us—even unto death on the cross. If you ever feel like you don't belong, think for a moment about God's legacy of pursuing *you*. You are His child, precious and adored.

The Old Testament is also a story of failure—not God's failure, but the failure on our side to uphold our part of the relational covenant. And yes, our failure continues in the New Testament. The disciples' lack of understanding; Judas' betrayal; Peter's denial of Jesus; the attempts to reinstitute the requirements of the law in the early church; Ananias and Sapphira; divisions among the early believers; the failures of the churches outlined in Revelation 2-3. It seems we, like Israel, fall more than we stand.

Despite our many, consistent failures, the Old and New Testaments are also a beautiful story of redemption—redemption from sin, yes, but also the redemption of our failures. God *never* gives up on us. He takes our failures and somehow works good through them. "And we know that all things work together for good for those who love God, who are called according to his purpose" (Romans 8:28 NET).

The Old and New Testaments are also a story of the faithfulness of the few—Caleb and Joshua, who were ready to enter the land of promise on Day 1; Jehoshaphat, who sent his army against three enemy armies with singers praising God in the lead; Shadrach, Meshach, and Abednego, willing to walk through the furnace for God whether He rescued them from the fire or not; Daniel, Ezekiel, and Jeremiah, all willing to speak God's truth no matter the consequences; Peter, once restored by Jesus, faithful to his death; Paul, after undergoing an extreme transformation, faithful through torture, imprisonment, and death; the list goes on.

The Scriptures also tell the story of the redemption of our dwelling place with God. Eden was God's original plan, a dwelling place with us on earth where He could walk with us in the garden in the cool of the day, where we could talk together always and enjoy our relationship, free from the presence of evil. But in order for the relationship to be one of love, He infused freedom of choice into the

DNA of the world, and in our freedom, we chose knowledge over love and infused the world with evil. (Another example of just how much our choices matter in the working out of God's will). Our intended dwelling place with God became tainted, wounded, and toxic for us—a place where evil battles against freedom and love and reviles our identities as children of God.

Enter Jesus. His first task was to remind us of the true nature of God by once again living among us, talking with us, teaching us, and enjoying relationship with us—the story of the gospels. His second task was to ransom us from captivity in evil's clutches and restore our freedom—the story of the cross. His third task was to remove the ultimate consequence of sin through the final defeat of death—the story of the resurrection.

His fourth task, which is ongoing, is to prepare our hearts and complete the restoration process of His dwelling place within us by reminding us of the truth of our identities as His beloved children. His final task, yet to be completed, is to reclaim and restore His dwelling place on earth, where He will return and gather us all to Himself, where once more we will walk and talk together as He intended in Eden.

While you wait in hopeful anticipation of His return, you aren't left as an orphan. His work within you and for you continues. He walks with you, and at times carries you, on the journey down the narrow path. He corrects your missteps and protects you when you stumble back onto the wide road. He busily tends His plantings of truth along the narrow way, while He continues to scrape away the old neural pathways. He reaches into the deepest places within you, the places even you can't see or reach, to loosen the grip of the sin nature, the root lie that you can be your own God, until He can at long last gently pull the root out.

Above all, God's love for His people is the primary theme paralleled in both the Old and New Testaments. I've already discussed how His love is seen in His patient, steadfast refusal to give up and His mercy and compassion offered Israel. His great and unfailing love is also touted in numerous psalms (Psalm 6:4, 13:5, 17:7, 18:50, 25:6, 26:3, 31:16, 32:10, 33:5, 18, 22, 36:7, 44:26, 48:9, 51:1, 52:8, 57:10, 62:12, 69:13, 85:7, 86:13, 89:1, 90:14, 94:18, 100:5, 103:8, 11, 17, 106:1, 45, 107:1, 8, 15, 21, 31, 108:4, 109:26, 117:2, 118:1-4, 29, 119:41, 76, 88, 130:7, 136:1-26, 138:2, 143:8, 12, 145:8, 147:11). I believe this list, from only one book in the Old Testament, makes the point.

The entire Song of Songs is a metaphor of God's love for His people. Even in Isaiah, a book challenging Israel to return to God, you read about God's deep love and compassion (Isaiah 54:10, 55:3, 63:9) and about God's love seen in the coming of Messiah (Isaiah 16:5, 53:5-12, 61:1-2). Because of His love, we are invited into His dwelling place ("I, by your great love, can come into your house" Psalm 5:7).

The cross, perhaps the greatest symbol of genuine love, is the central story of the New Testament. Rather than try to list all the verses proclaiming God's love in the New Testament, I will highlight a few key verses which mirror the descriptions of His love throughout the Bible. John 3:16, of course, gives the reason for the cross: "for God so loved the world"—as does John 15:13 ("Greater love has no one than this: to lay down one's life for one's friends") and Romans 5:8 "But God demonstrates his own love for us in this: While we were still sinners, Christ died for us").

Paul's prayer for the Ephesians was for them to truly comprehend God's love: "I pray that you, being rooted and established in love, may have power, together with all the Lord's holy people, to grasp how wide and long and high and deep is the love of Christ, and to know this love that surpasses knowledge—that you may be filled to the measure of all the fullness of God" (Ephesian 3:17-19). Notice Paul's description of God's love as surpassing knowledge—this statement explains that His love stands in direct opposition to the sin of Eden. He goes on to call us "dearly loved children" (Ephesians 5:1).

Romans 8:35-39 states nothing can separate us from His great love. Colossians 3:12 calls us, "God's chosen people, holy and dearly loved." I Timothy 1:14 says His grace, faith, and love are "poured out" abundantly on us. And one of my favorite exclamations of God's love is found in I John 3:1: "See what great love the Father has lavished on us, that we should be called children of God!"

Do you hear the zeal, the abundance, the unsurpassed greatness of His love? His patience, devotion, and respect for you can be overwhelming in its generosity and magnitude. He loves you with a passion and desire you can't imagine—unless you experience it firsthand.

Experiencing God

All these words sound good, but they are just that—words—conveying concepts or ideas—without the *experience* of its power. (Thus, the reason for Paul's fervent prayer in Ephesians 3:17-19).

So, how do you access this experience?

If feeling the breadth and depth of His love is something you crave, there is good news. He craves sharing His love with you as much as you desire to feel it. Sometimes, things get in the way, like our busyness, our focus on the worldly, or the lies we believe, but if you seek His presence and are patient, I believe you will find Him meeting you there. I've listed below some intentional things you can do to open yourself up for the experience of God's presence and love.

1. Spend time in silence with Jesus. Clear your mind of distractions by meditating on a verse that's meaningful to you or recalling a time you've heard from Him previously. Then slow and deepen your breathing, center yourself in your heart instead of your head, and wait for a while to see what "floats" up from your heart. Follow whatever comes up, as long as it produces peace in your heart.

2. Make a habit of "checking in" with Jesus numerous times throughout the day. It doesn't have to be lengthy or formal—just a quick, "How are we doing? Anything you want to tell me?" for a couple of minutes. It's particularly good while you are driving in the car to turn off the podcasts or music

and have a conversation as if He's sitting in the passenger seat with you. This new habit is to get you used to the idea of His constant presence.

3. Find a prayer partner, someone who has a relational connection with Jesus, and ask them to spend some time once or twice a week seeking His presence with you. Sometimes, another person can discern what's in the way when you can't see it. It also empowers our prayers to pray in community, with two or more gathered.

4. When you find yourself in the middle of an emotional response (a time when you are already connected to your heart), ask Him to meet you in the emotion. It can be a strong positive or negative emotion. Try not to step out of the emotion to talk to Him, though. Remain, as best you can, centered in the experience of your feelings. Look for His presence, whether through images, words, or impressions on your heart.

5. Pay attention to your responses. When you are moved to compassion or tears, when you feel a deep sense of contentment or peace, when you experience love for someone like your child or spouse, or when you feel great joy, ascribe those feelings to the presence of His Spirit within you and consciously choose to share the experience with Him.

These are just a few suggestions, to try to give you a starting place for deepening your relational experience with Jesus. As you attempt to experience Him, just know that He loves you with an unfathomable love, and, like the children of Israel, He will never leave you, forsake you, or give up on you, *no matter what.* Just like Israel, you are His, and no one—nothing—can separate you from His love.

Consider This

1. Compare your life experiences with those of the Israelites in slavery in Egypt. How has God come for you and rescued you from your own form of "slavery"? In what ways has He "brought you out" and parted the waters in your life so you can be free?

2. What questions have you asked God about the effectiveness of your identity for what He has called you to do?

3. When have fear (e.g., 'what if' questions) and shame or blame (e.g., self-judgment or accusations against God) and discouragement (e.g., giving up) hindered you on your journey with God?

4. What "idols" have you had in your life (either past or present)? What have you sacrificed because of those idols?

5. What are some times in your life you've experienced difficulty, and because of fear, you avoided it rather than face it? What are some times you've faced struggles and walked through them with God? How did each time turn out for you?

6. Think about God's description of the Israelites as "stiff-necked." How does the sin nature evidence itself in you?

7. In what circumstances have you had these or similar responses: *I want what I want when I want it; I'll follow you, as long as—; what have you done for me lately?; I can protect myself if I anticipate the worst possible outcomes because then I won't be surprised or disappointed; this is hard—surely it would be better to go back?*

8. I suggest comparing your story to the story of Israel and list several "have you ever" questions for you to consider. Which questions did you answer, "yes"? Which questions did you answer "no"? How did it feel to do this comparison?

9. What kinds of "altars" have you built in your "temple"? Which "foreign gods" have you agreed to worship?

10. In what ways do you operate as an alien and foreigner in this world? How do you feel about not being of the world?

11. Where have you felt like you belonged? Have you felt you belong in the Kingdom and in your dwelling place with God? What gets in the way of that sense of belonging?

12. What fruit do you see of worldly values in your life? What fruit do you see of Kingdom values in your life? How has the enemy distorted positive values and turned them away from the Kingdom in your experience?

13. Where has thinking in extremes (black and white, legalistic thinking) impacted your life, either in yourself or in someone else in your sphere?

14. Where have you seen God's beautiful redemption in your life? In what ways does He remind you of your true identity?

15. How would you describe your experience of God's love?

Submission is not simply giving up, it is aligning.

We must relinquish methods we've tried to build upon — control, performance, shame, fear, justifications, excuses, indifference and avoidance of responsibility.

CHAPTER THREE
THE MATERIALS

You may believe Jesus begins His work in your heart when you invite Jesus to enter, but don't forget He said He goes *before* you to prepare your heart to be His dwelling place. He has been at work in you from the moment of your creation. Just like the Israelites, He has pursued you your whole life.

At your inception, God provides certain raw materials for the building process. Through the process of living your life, you collect some additional materials which you bring to the construction site for the project, and some of those things you've collected and stored must be cleared out to make way for the new construction. All of God's materials are vital to the preparation of the dwelling place. The same cannot be said for all of the materials you provide.

God provides you with a portion of the material for the foundation of the dwelling—your true identity, the reflection of God's nature He placed within you. This identity is made up of aspects of His nature He selected specifically and intentionally to "knit" into your DNA.

You are exactly who He designed you to be. You are, completely and totally, who God wants you to be in your true nature, and that nature is sufficient. However, because you are not God—having only those aspects of His nature He placed within you—your nature is not complete.

While your identity is a key element of the home's foundation, it can't hold up the building alone. Imagine trying to build a foundation with just sand without the cement, gravel, and water. Yes, sand is sufficient as sand, and it is a necessary component to make the foundation, but without the other elements, the sand is blown away in the wind. In the same way, Jesus must join with your identity—the two must be made one—for the foundation to be complete. "So this is what the Sovereign LORD says: 'See, I lay a stone in Zion, a tested stone, a precious cornerstone for a sure foundation'" (Isaiah 28:16).

Jesus is the cornerstone and the mortar for your foundation. Your dwelling was never meant to stand without it.

So, you bring the identity God provides within you—and Jesus brings the rest. As the farmer, the one who tends the soil, He scrapes away the old paths (Matthew 13:4), fills in where the soil is shallow (Matthew 13:5), clears away the weeds and thorns (Matthew 13:7), and readies the ground for planting good seeds. Your premade paths won't allow for His seeds of truth to take root. Your internal clutter interferes with His plantings, and your lies choke out your growth. None of these materials you bring to the project can remain if the foundation is to be strong and secure.

The nature of the foundation determines the integrity, stability, and design of the house. Think about your worldly home. What would happen to it if the foundation was broken or incomplete—or made with only sand? As Jesus explained, "As for everyone who comes to me and hears my words and puts them into practice, I will show you what they are like. They are like a man building a house, who dug down deep and laid the foundation on rock. When a flood came, the torrent struck that house but could not shake it, because it was well built. But the one who hears my words and does not put them into practice is like a man who built a house on the ground without a foundation. The moment the torrent struck that house, it collapsed and its destruction was complete" (Luke 6:47-49).

To build your foundation, you must "dig down deep" within you with Jesus and allow Him to establish Himself as the Rock on which everything else is built. But what does He mean by "dig down deep"?

If you are honest in your evaluation, you will likely admit that most of your life is lived on the surface. We spend the majority of our time in routines—we eat, we sleep, we work—wash, rinse, repeat. Even our respites from routine often exist on the surface level, something akin to going to a movie or a game night with friends. We focus on the momentary enjoyment—and there's nothing wrong with having those times. Examine, though, how comparatively little time you spend "digging deep"—going beyond the superficial into depth of feeling, depth of insight, or depth of wisdom. (If you say, "Not very often," you are like most people).

When you snorkel along the surface of the ocean, it's very pleasant. You receive the enjoyment of the sun, the water, and occasionally, a sea creature who comes up to your visual range to check out what is swimming above them. Oh, but when you dive down deep, you enter another world. Your mind is stimulated anew by the myriad colors and sights and new experiences. You really "come alive" as you are filled with awe and wonder at everything that surrounds you.

Digging down deep with Jesus is like scuba diving into your own heart and soul and spirit. He awakens you with fresh insights into yourself, others, and Him. He enlivens you with new understanding of His glory expressed within you. He opens up your mind and heart to receive His love in a new way. He fills you with powerful truths that blast away the remnants of dirt and detritus from your sin nature. And He establishes a foundation on which you can build a beautiful life.

The key to digging down deep is doing it with Jesus. Doing it alone would be like night diving without a light—you'd have no idea where you were going, and you'd see nothing. Simply put, you can't know what you don't know. You need His light to reveal what you cannot see on your own. What feels true to you isn't necessarily true. What you think you know about yourself, you may be surprised to find is a distortion of your reality or worse.

To dig down deep, you must penetrate beyond the "covering" the world has used to obscure your true nature. You must enter boldly into your hiding places with illumination that reveals them for what they are—prisons of your own design. You must be willing for Jesus to tear down all the walls and protections you've put in place to try to retain your illusion of control, so you can see beyond them into the true spirit within you. You must bear a fierce and honest evaluation of the state of your heart and be willing to open it up for growth and change.

As you dig down deep—which is a process, not a one-time act—Jesus unites with you to create your foundation on the Rock (Himself) at your core.

If all of these things sound intimidating or difficult to you, consider this: whether you choose to dig down deep or not, Jesus is already there, working to establish His foundation within you. It's not like you are exposing your deep, dark secrets to Him. He already knows them and has known them since time began. As He stated, He goes *before* you to prepare your dwelling place. So, you may as well join Him. Thankfully, He carries the bulk of the load.

Think about how the foundation establishes the size and form of your earthly home. Without a foundation, your home would sprawl in random, discordant, and chaotic shapes, with no order or structure to hold it all together or give it function and purpose. The same is true of your life. If you build your life without a strong foundation, your life will become a rambling, muddled mess, with no clarity of purpose or meaning—directionless and insecure.

Finally, consider how shaky a house without a foundation would be. Without proper support, the walls would shift and bow, causing cracks, gaps, and crumbling plaster. The roof would sag and buckle. Ultimately, the house will fall.

But a house with a strong foundation will withstand the ravages of weather and time. The builders know how to construct the floorplan based on the foundation. The walls and roof have a secure anchor. No matter the "storm," the house continues to stand, stable and secure on its firm foundation. "God's solid foundation stands firm, sealed with this inscription: 'The Lord knows those who are His'" (II Timothy 2:19).

Counting the Cost

You need to know, it's costly to build the kind of dwelling Jesus calls us to create in partnership with Him, one with a sure foundation and Kingdom materials used in the construction. In fact, we are told to "estimate the cost" to make sure we have enough within us to complete the project, lest we be ridiculed for our failure to complete it (Luke 14:27-29). We spend many years of our lives building up our own structure—our illusions, judgments, hierarchies, and deceptions—but our structure *must be torn down* to make way for God's dwelling within us. Often, the tearing down is painful and the letting go is difficult, even torturous.

The self as God illusion—the Edenic belief that we can be like God, which is the foundation on which we build our self-made structure—needs to be demolished. Our efforts to "break" the false foundation will fall short. The structure is too entrenched in us. We can never fully see or understand all of its far-reaching tentacles, snaking throughout our lives and burrowing into our cells. Only in *partnership and agreement* with Jesus can the false foundation be destroyed.

How, then, is the old foundation broken? Like Jehoshaphat, we approach God in humility and acknowledge, "For we have no power... We do not know what to do, but our eyes are on you" (II Chronicles 20:12). To this prayer, God responds, "Do not be afraid or discouraged...For the battle is not yours, but God's" (v. 15). This is our partnership with God—true humility, acknowledging God is God and we are not, and acceptance of our powerlessness against the lie of self as God.

As Isaiah 28:15 describes, we have, "entered into a covenant with death, with the realm of the dead we have made an agreement...we have made a lie our refuge and falsehood our hiding place." Our agreement with God takes the form of breaking our agreement with death and agreeing to rely on Him instead of on our own self-aggrandizing devices. We accept Jesus as our "precious cornerstone for a sure foundation" (v. 16) by allowing His presence and truth to "sweep away (our) refuge, the lie, and water (to) overflow (our) hiding place" (v. 17).

In His loving kindness, Jesus will never force partnership and agreement with Him against our will. Our God-given freedom allows us that choice—and if we choose otherwise, Jesus will allow us to remain in our self-constructed hiding place atop our false foundation unto death, even though it breaks His heart. But, when we partner with Jesus and agree to rely on Him, He promises, "to rescue us from the present evil age, according to the will of our God and Father" (Galatians 1:4) and "from the dominion of darkness" (Colossians 1:13) to bring us into His Kingdom (v. 13).

Once our self as God illusion is broken, our other lies and judgments tend to crumble. Unfortunately, those aspects of our structure often guard the false foundation and make it difficult for us to willingly agree for our foundation to be demolished, so sometimes we must partner with Jesus to stand against other materials in our structure before He can get to its base.

For example, we may cling to our *walls* of self-protection and self-defense with vehemence, refusing to let them go at all costs. These defenses are rooted in a lack of trust in God's protection—often based on the lie that God's protection takes the form of *prevention* instead of presence, which is rooted in a belief in *control*—another illusion. Control then anchors itself in our self-as-God belief. Do you see how intertwined and convoluted our false structure can be? No wonder we need God's help!

We may also cling to pillars of *judgments* against ourselves, and these judgments pour out of us toward others and turn into hierarchical views of "better than/worse than" and "greater than/less than," building *levels* into our structure where we measure ourselves in comparison to others according to our judgments. In this way, we lose our true sense of self based on who God says we are.

When we judge ourselves, we judge others in the same way. Our belief in hierarchical judgments projects onto others. We see those around us through the lenses of the judgments we've made against ourselves. These judgments also pour out against God, leaving us with a sense of God as distant and unreachable—and unloving. These judgments against God may also be bound into the illusion of control, if we believe we can work hard enough to be "good enough" for God's love, as if we "make" God love us by earning it. The same thing can happen in our relationships with others, as we try to "make" people love us by being good enough, or we demand people be good enough for us to love.

Shame is another lie we may hold in a tight grip, under the illusion that it is a *ceiling* to shield us from exposure. Shame, we believe, hides our failings and sin, when in reality it only keeps us bound to the sin, so we continue in those same behaviors, pulled deeper and deeper into the hole we are digging. Shame also leaves us feeling separated from God, and although Scripture tells us nothing can separate us from the love of God in Christ Jesus (Romans 8:38-39), we *feel* separated from Him and His love beneath the covering of shame.

We also use fear to make the *roof* of our structure. Fear is directly connected to the illusion of control. We convince ourselves that listening to fear keeps us from getting hurt by anticipating all negatives—something we cannot know, because we can't know the future. In reality, much like shame binds us to the harmful behaviors it claims to hide, listening to fear creates the opposite outcome from what we truly desire, as we unconsciously create what we most fear. Also, research shows that people who focus on negatives are more prone to depression and anxiety.

At this point, you might be thinking, "Wait, fear is a good thing! Isn't it fear that keeps us from doing harmful or dangerous things?" In truth, wisdom is what keeps us from pursuing something dangerous or harmful. Wisdom and fear are not the same thing. Fear is based on unknowns—in other words, we don't know what will happen, so we fear it. Wisdom, however, is based on understanding. We don't put our hands on the stove because we *understand* it will burn us. We don't walk down the middle of a busy highway because we *understand* we are in danger of being hit by a car. While wisdom is a part of God's Kingdom, fear is not. "There is no fear in love. But perfect love drives out fear" (I John 4:18).

We *furnish* our structure with justifications, excuses, regrets, denial, bitterness, rationalizations, resentments, unforgiveness, and avoidance of responsibility. Like a hoarder, we clutter our structure with these stumbling blocks to receiving God's healing, and we don't want to let them go. Each one throws up another obstacle as Jesus seeks to break us free from our false foundation.

We've spent a lot of time and effort in the construction of our structure. Even though the structure becomes a prison for us, we may feel a sense of loss when Jesus wants to tear it down—the loss of our investment and the loss of our illusion of control. Like the Israelites, we may want to turn back to Egypt rather than sacrifice the contents and materials of our self-designed dwelling place.

Whatever sacrifices we must make, whatever losses we must incur, God asks us to commit fully to the new project. He calls us to go "all in" on its completion. This means we can't hold onto those old lies we view as life preservers anymore. We can't keep the roof of fear or the ceiling of shame as our covering. We must be willing for Jesus to tear down the pillars of judgment we use to hold up our structure. And our walls of self-protection, which hold everyone—including God—at a distance must come down.

We can't keep revisiting our old neural pathways, replowing the old ground we've walked on the wide paths—not if we want the kind of dwelling God desires to provide for us. As Scripture admonishes, we can't "pour new wine into old wineskins" (Matthew 9:17). "Otherwise, the wine will burst the skins, and both the wine and the wineskins will be ruined" (Mark 2:22). In the same way, we can't bring our transformed selves into our old ways. The structure of our old ways will infect us and destroy the progress Jesus has achieved.

We must be willing to let go of all of our old materials and purchase the treasures of God to build our dwelling with Him. As Paul explains, "if anyone is in Christ, the new creation has come: The old has gone, the new is here!" (II Corinthians 5:17). You can't live with the old materials and bring in the new construction. If you do, the foundation will fail, and the building will collapse.

Brought to Light

In case you thought it doesn't matter what kinds of materials you use to build on your foundation, Scripture is clear: your materials matter. "For no one can lay any foundation other than the one already laid, which is Jesus Christ. If anyone builds on this foundation using gold, silver, costly stones, wood, hay or straw, their work will be shown for what it is, because the Day will bring it to light. It will be revealed with fire, and the fire will test the quality of each person's work. If what has been built survives, the builder will receive a reward. If it is burned up, the builder will suffer loss but yet will be saved—even though only as one escaping through the flames" (I Corinthians 3:11-15).

These verses have been interpreted as indicating the works we do for God will be rewarded, and we will be punished for not doing good works for God. But Jesus' own words contradict this interpretation: "'Do not work for food that spoils, but for food that endures to eternal life, which the Son of Man will give you. For on him God the Father has placed his seal of approval.' Then they asked him, 'What must we do to do the works God requires?' Jesus answered, 'The work of God is this: to believe in the one he has sent'" (John 6:27-29).

Paul also denies the efficacy of works for achieving righteousness, saying, "If, in fact, Abraham was justified by works, he had something to boast about—but not before God. What does Scripture say? 'Abraham believed God, and it was credited to him as righteousness.' Now to the one who works, wages are not credited as a gift but as an obligation. However, to the one who does not work but trusts God who justifies the ungodly, their faith is credited as righteousness. David says the same thing when he speaks of the blessedness of the one to whom God credits righteousness apart from works" (Romans 4:2-6); and again, "For it is by grace you have been saved, through faith—and this is not from yourselves, it is the gift of God—not by works, so that no one can boast" (Ephesians 2:8-9).

So, if I Corinthians 3:11-15 doesn't reference the works we do for God, what is it saying? Paul speaks specifically about the quality of what we build upon the foundation laid in us (which is Christ). In other words, what materials do *we* bring to the construction of our dwelling place? The building project is, after all, a partnership with Jesus.

As we make choices based on faith (acceptance and trust leading to action) and follow Jesus as our partner, we build together a dwelling place for the Kingdom of God within us, for where He lives, God's Kingdom is present. ("Don't you know that you yourselves are God's temple and that God's Spirit dwells in your midst?" — I Corinthians 3:16). These I Corinthians verses are asking what materials we will use to build that internal dwelling *with and for Jesus* and telling us that our materials will be revealed for what they are come the light of the Day.

I mentioned earlier we need to build our dwelling with the treasures of God, and that those who have built with the so-called treasures of the world will have to shed those materials before entering their dwelling in heaven. The "fire" which will test the quality of our materials will burn up anything not of the Kingdom. The journey to our heavenly dwelling place is determined by what we bring with us—the more Kingdom materials we bring, the less we need to collect on our journey.

So, "wood, hay, and straw" represent those worldly building materials, all of which will be burned up in the purifying fires of God. Gold, silver, and costly stones, however, are *refined* by the fire. As Scripture states: "I will refine them like silver and test them like gold. They will call on my name and I will answer them; I will say, 'They are my people,' and they will say, 'The LORD is our God'" (Zechariah

13:9); and "For He will be like a refiner's fire. He will sit as a refiner and purifier of silver" (Malachi 3:2-3).

Rather than these verses being fear-provoking, in anticipation of punishment—for as I John 4:18 says, "fear has to do with punishment"—these verses present an opportunity, our chance to choose our building materials wisely. These verses also encourage us, letting us know we will be saved, even if our building materials are of the world and burn up upon entry into heaven. Of course, the urging is to build with costly Kingdom materials, so we won't be "as one escaping through the flames."

Sowing and reaping are Kingdom principles (Matthew 13:3-40; Galatians 6:7-8; James 3:17-18). What we sow, we reap (Galatians 6:7), and how and where we sow matters in what grows in us and what is produced for the Kingdom (Matthew 13:3-40). Will you sow weeds or good seed? Will your treasure be collected for the Kingdom, or will it be wood, hay, and straw, burned up in the fire? Will your harvest be "first of all pure; then peace-loving, considerate, submissive, full of mercy and good fruit, impartial and sincere" (James 3:17) and "righteousness" (v. 18), or will everything you've planted be snatched away, choked out, or wither and die?

If "the wisdom that comes from heaven" (v. 17) produces these fruits, and wisdom is based on understanding, God has provided us with everything we need to know in order to build a dwelling with and for Jesus that will survive the fire. Throughout Scripture, He describes His Kingdom treasures and urges us to "seek first His Kingdom and His righteousness" (Matthew 6:33) in every choice we make.

Inheritance

Jesus has given us "an inheritance that can never perish, spoil, or fade" (I Peter 1:4). "This inheritance is kept in heaven for you, who through faith are shielded by God's power until the coming of the salvation that is ready to be revealed in the last time" (v. 4-5). Our inheritance is "the kingdom prepared for you since the creation of the world" (Matthew 25:34), an inheritance based on God's promise (Galatians 3:18). It is an inheritance guaranteed with the seal of the Holy Spirit (Ephesians 1:13-14). You are promised a place at the banquet table of God to share in His great feast (Luke 13:29). But know this: you cannot bring spoiled "food" to the banquet table, any more than you can bring immoral, impure, or idolatrous thoughts into the Kingdom (Ephesians 5:5). In the same way, you cannot build your Kingdom dwelling with materials that perish.

What, then, are the Kingdom materials He provides for you to build your Kingdom dwelling together? I've already described how the dwelling's foundation is built on the union of your identity with Jesus Christ. This identity is your original creation, without all the overlays of worldly materials you've used to build up your own structure; thus, Jesus' admonition that to enter the Kingdom, you must become as a little child (Matthew 18:3, 19:14).

Throughout His ministry, Jesus presented in great detail the qualities of one inheriting the Kingdom. The Sermon on the Mount begins with the quality, "poor in spirit" (Matthew 5:3). This doesn't mean demeaning yourself or being self-debasing, nor does it refer to denying yourself God's spiritual treasures (Matthew 6:21). Jesus is referring to genuine humility, defined as the radical acceptance that "God is God, and I am not." He means the Edenic self as God lie is dead, culled from you like cancer is cut from the body to restore health. I find it interesting that He chose to first address the removal of the Edenic lie as a prerequisite for Kingdom inheritance in His most important sermon. As I stated earlier, all other lie beliefs and judgments are rooted in that foundation.

Jesus also mentions righteousness in two contexts in the same sermon: first, those who hunger and thirst for righteousness are promised to be filled (v. 6), and then, those who are persecuted because of their righteousness will inherit the Kingdom of heaven (v. 10). He also said, "unless your righteousness surpasses that of the Pharisees and the teachers of the law, you will certainly not enter the kingdom of heaven" (v. 20).

But how can anyone surpass the righteousness of the teachers of the law? Who is truly righteous? "No one," according to Psalm 14:1, 53:1, and Paul in Romans 3:10, speaking of those under the law. He goes on to say, "righteousness is given through *faith* in Jesus Christ to all who believe" (v. 22). So, when we, in faith, hunger and thirst for Jesus, we hunger and thirst for righteousness, and we will be "filled," meaning made righteous by His righteousness. Remember, it is our oneness with Him that completes our Kingdom foundation.

And when we are persecuted—wronged, mistreated, oppressed, harassed, tormented, bullied, intimidated, singled out, baited, discriminated against—because of our faith in Jesus, we receive the Kingdom inheritance. This result isn't because of the persecution itself, but because it means we've chosen Jesus over acceptance by the world. We're willing to sacrifice worldly good for the greater portion.

Jesus also said we must be "born again," or "born of water and the Spirit" to enter the Kingdom (John 3:3-5). He goes on to explain, "Flesh gives birth to flesh, but the Spirit gives birth to spirit" (v. 6). Similarly, Paul states, "And just as we have borne the image of the earthly man, so shall we bear the image of the heavenly man. I declare to you, brothers and sisters, that flesh and blood cannot inherit the kingdom of God, nor does the perishable inherit the imperishable" (I Corinthians 15:49-50). Our spirits must be born anew, transformed into Christ's likeness (Galatians 3:26-27; I John 3:2) by the presence of the Holy Spirit within us, the Holy Spirit who is the deposit guaranteeing our inheritance (Ephesians 1:13-14).

"Those who belong to Christ Jesus have crucified the flesh with its passions and desires. Since we live by the Spirit, let us keep in step with the Spirit" (Galatians 5:24-25). So, in addition to being born anew through the Holy Spirit, those who inherit the Kingdom live by the Spirit and follow His lead. Similarly, we are told whoever practices and teaches God's commandments will be great in the Kingdom (Matthew

5:19), and those who do the will of God will enter the Kingdom (7:21). Our focus is not to be on worldly desires but on the things of the Spirit—the ways of the Kingdom.

What does it mean to live by the Spirit? Scripture says the Kingdom of God is given to those who produce its fruit, the fruit of the Spirit (Matthew 21:43). As we walk in concert with His Spirit, listening for His leading and guidance while refusing to pursue the desires of the flesh/sin nature, we'll find our true, created nature becomes unhindered—free to flow from us into the world—and our choices produce good fruit both in us and in others, and the Kingdom of God is furthered on earth.

What does it mean to do the will of God? According to Jesus, the answer is simple: love. When asked to identify the most important commandments, Jesus answered, "Love the Lord your God with all your heart and with all your soul and with all your mind and with all your strength. The second is this: Love your neighbor as yourself" (Mark 12:30-31). And when one of the teachers of the law agreed with Jesus, saying these two commands are more important than all the offerings and sacrifices, Jesus replied, "You are not far from the Kingdom of God" (v. 34). When we make our choices based on the answer to the question, "What is the loving thing to do?" we are doing God's will. Again, these choices will produce good fruit.

So, God provides the raw materials of humility, righteousness, faith, sacrifice, transformation, the fruit of the Spirit, and love to build our Kingdom dwelling within us. These materials supplant our own structures of pride, iniquity, malice, doubt, self-indulgence, self-absorption, and worldly desires. These materials of the flesh are temporal, but God's materials are eternal, "a spring of water welling up to eternal life" (John 4:14). We need never hunger or thirst again.

Innate Materials

In addition to your specific, unique identity, the nature God wove into you, and the raw materials God brings to the construction of your dwelling, He has provided some basic materials innate to all human beings. Like your identity, these materials reflect God's character, as you will see, for we witness these qualities in Jesus. These materials are also important to the design of your Kingdom dwelling, as they are aspects of what makes us human.

As a result, the lies and judgments adopted from the world often pervert and hinder the expression of these qualities, and the deceptions of the enemy can twist these qualities into something opposite from what God intended. For example, our desire for significance and purpose can be twisted into a belief that our identity is found in what we do rather than who we are created to be. It's important, then, that we maintain our partnership with God in our expression of each of these qualities to prevent their perversion.

Infants are born with the ability to trust. A neurological "post" exists in the brain before birth where trust is located. A baby emerges from the womb trusting they will be fed. They trust the mother's care, until some action or circumstance teaches them otherwise. Mistrust, like all other lie beliefs, is learned, not innate. In building trust into the structure of our brains, God lays the foundation for our trust in Him to grow.

Every infant is also born with a propensity to explore. We wonder at the things we don't understand and are curious about the things we don't know. God built in this desire for exploration to facilitate our growth, development, and understanding. Our desire to seek is highly valued by God and is how we ultimately find God. He even instructs us to seek (Matthew 6:33, 7:7-8, John 7:18, plus countless verses in the Old Testament admonishing to seek God) and describes Himself as a seeker (Malachi 2:15, Luke 19:10, John 5:30, 8:50).

Our exploration can take many forms—learning about something new, delving into the study of Scripture, journeying to a new place and experiencing its beauty, changing jobs, seeing experiences with fresh eyes, forming new relationships, even diving deep into our own hearts to understand better who we are and what elements within us Jesus needs to clear out. But to prevent exploration from becoming about self-gratification instead of growth, we need to include Jesus on our exploring journeys. The more we explore with Jesus as our partner, the more we understand, and the more we understand, the greater our Godly wisdom.

One of the reasons our self-protective structures are so damaging is their hindrance of our natural desire to explore, stunting our growth and limiting our understanding. Growth requires movement, and our drive to explore motivates our movement. Through exploration, we learn to face challenges and difficulties with courage. We learn perseverance, which builds character (Romans 5:3-4). We face our fears instead of succumbing to them and allowing them to dictate our choices. Those who embrace this intrinsic desire to explore are generally happier, have greater life satisfaction, and find more meaning in life.

We are also created for adventure. Our desires for mastery, excitement, new sensations, and challenging experiences drive our need for adventure. This need can be easily perverted, however, if our desire for adventure isn't paired with wisdom. Remember, wisdom is based on Godly understanding and produces good fruit, where fear is directed toward the unknown. Fear can stunt the expressions of our desire for adventure, while a lack of wisdom can turn adventure-seeking into risk-taking behavior that leads to self-harm. Neither of these responses are in alignment with God's desires.

Certainly, calling the Kingdom of God a grand adventure would be selling it way short, but living in the Kingdom is a new and challenging experience filled with excitement and new sensations every day, for the rest of our lives. The disciples were called by Jesus to embark on a great adventure with Him, one of great joy and meaning but also fraught with peril. Their adventure was not common thrill-seeking; instead, it was driven by a deep purpose, something that God also imbedded in our natures.

Deep in our hearts, we all desire a purpose. We want to feel like we have significance—that we matter and have a meaningful, lasting impact. God not only gives us this desire, He also provides us the single most important purpose anyone can have—to return the Kingdom of God to earth and restore God's original design to its full expression.

We are called to this grand adventure, as the disciples were, and as followers of Christ, it is our driving purpose, our reason for being, and our eternal significance. Every expression of your true nature, which reflects Christ's nature into the world, reclaims spiritual ground and moves us closer to the Kingdom's restoration. It's also important to realize that every time we indulge the flesh/sin nature and hide our true selves, we are hindering the Kingdom's return. I will say it again: our choices have great significance.

Our identity and our significance are integrally intertwined; however, we can't allow an external purpose to supplant our identity as what defines us. Many people live their lives believing their job or their children define them—and when those things go away, which they will, they are left bereft and void of a sense of purpose. We are not what we *do*. We are who God created us to *be*. Our primary purpose, to usher in the Kingdom of God, depends not on what we do in this life but on whether we are being our true selves as we do it.

God has implanted in us both creativity and imagination, so that we might partner with Him in the creative process. We also need creativity and imagination for other reasons. Imagination is essential in making decisions—the ability to imagine potential outcomes and consequences makes for effective decision makers. Problem solving also requires the ability to imagine potentialities and consequences, and create multiple possible solutions, all from what we imagine in our minds.

God also offers us creativity as one of the ways we experience joy and connection with Him. When an artist captures a beautiful sunset on canvas, a musician perfects a moving chorus that touches people's spirits, a writer turns a phrase that communicates an emotion or a scene exactly as they visualize it, a scientist helps discover a cure for a fatal disease, or a mother births a precious baby, they each touch the edges of God's experience as our Creator and connect with God's heart. In some small way, we get a taste of His joy in His creation as we create.

Our desire to love and be loved is one of the greatest gifts God has provided in our inmost being. The most important fruit of the Spirit is love. Without love, we become "depraved minds" (II Timothy 3:3, 8), —and "without fruit and uprooted—twice dead" (Jude 1:12). Paul calls love "the greatest of these" (I Corinthians 13:13). Jesus synthesized all of the law and prophets into one word—love (Mark 12:29-32). In fact, God's essence—His very nature—is love (I John 4:8).

Therefore, we desire connection, specifically connection with our Creator. A part of our brain, the parietal cortex, is where we experience transcendent communion with God and awareness of a being greater than ourselves, as well as where we experience awareness of self and process sensation and language. Look at the confluence of things that are centered in this part of the brain. Our awareness of ourselves is directly connected (or at least co-occurring) with our experience of God. Processing language and sensation—elements crucial for communication and relationship—are also involved in this same brain area. I find it amazing that God designed our brains with all the elements needed for a real and meaningful relationship with God (an ability to experience God, to transcend ourselves, to commune with God, to talk with God and understand His responses, to sense the higher realm, and to be aware of our own being and nature) located in the same area.

Joy is directly connected to giving and receiving love. Without love, we have no joy, and without joy, we become bitter and hopeless, withering from within like desiccating fruit in a drought. Worship, the expression of our love for God, is filled with expressions of joy—in song and shouts and dancing, as described throughout the Psalms. And we know Jesus experienced joy, because it was "for the joy set before Him He endured the cross, scorning its shame" (Hebrews 12:2). He is described in Luke 10:21 as "full of joy through the Holy Spirit." Speaking of remaining in God's love, Jesus said, "I have told you this so that my joy may be in you and that your joy may be complete" (John 15:11).

God also gives us an innate desire for freedom. God desires that "creation itself will be liberated from its bondage to decay and brought into the freedom and glory of the children of God" (Romans 8:21). II Corinthians 3:17 tells us "where the Spirit of the Lord is, there is freedom." Messiah is prophesied to "proclaim freedom for the captives and release from darkness for the prisoners" (Isaiah 61:1), which Jesus accomplished by His death on the cross and His resurrection. So, not only is freedom God's desire and the result of His Spirit's presence, it is also the reason for Christ's coming.

My favorite verse in Scripture is Galatians 5:1, "It is for freedom that Christ has set us free." The freedom He purchased for me by paying the ransom to release me from bondage is valuable beyond measure and is something I hold dear to my heart and guard with fierce vehemence. With God's help, as much as I am able, I will not allow anyone or anything to steal my freedom and return me to captivity! Freedom in Christ means freedom from fear and shame, freedom from slavery to the flesh, freedom to love from a pure heart, freedom to express your true nature in its fullness, and freedom to build your inner dwelling place and your future Kingdom home, filled with His treasures. What a glorious freedom He has provided for us!

We are called to be free (Galatians 5:13) and to live as free people (I Peter 2:16), but we are also warned, "do not use your freedom as a cover-up for evil" (v. 16) or to "indulge the flesh" (Galatians 5:13). From these warnings, you can tell how our God-given freedom could be perverted into an excuse for sinning. As Paul warns, "What shall we say, then? Shall we go on sinning so that grace may increase? By no means! We are those who have died to sin; how can we live in it any longer? For we know that our old self was crucified with him so that the body ruled by sin might be done away with, that we should no longer be slaves to sin—because anyone who has died has been set free from sin." (Romans 6:1-2, 6-7).

Many feel like the Romans and Galatians, that freedom means a loss of control. Remember, however—*control is an illusion.* How can something that is an illusion be lost? Instead of producing out of control behavior, freedom expands to maximum capacity your ability to choose. Freedom removes the external limits imposed on your free will choices. Freedom doesn't mean you will no longer choose wisely; it just means you can choose from all possible choices. Certainly, wise, Godly choices are still among the possible choices you can make.

Continuing to sin or indulging the flesh only makes us slaves to sin again, robbing our hard-won freedom from us. Remember, seeking out God's precepts produces freedom (Psalm 119:45). If we are to fully experience the wonderful freedom He has provided for us, we'll want to refuse the flesh/sin nature and choose to stay away from all things not of His Kingdom.

Clearing Away the Old Materials

As we talk about the perversion of God's materials, it's important to remember this truth: the judgments of the world are lies (meaning they are not real, not true, don't exist in reality) and the deceptions of the enemy are smoke-and-mirrors (illusions, tricks, sleight of hand, misdirection, mirages, artifices). Just like a magician's illusion, you have to buy the lie to be fooled by it, but when you know the trick of it, it's clear to see that it's false. In other words, we cannot be deceived without our cooperation.

The enemy has no real power, just the ability to deceive, and if we stand strong in the truth, he is rendered powerless. We must agree to believe his deceptions, or they are revealed for the illusions they are. Without our agreement, they're harmless, like telling me that a chunk of mud is a piece of chocolate. If I know what mud is and clearly see the object before me is wet dirt, and I know what chocolate looks like, I'll simply refuse to eat it! Only someone who doesn't know what chocolate is or doesn't recognize mud can be fooled. Having God's truth written on our hearts and minds (Hebrews 8:10, 10:16) then, is paramount. Otherwise, we are vulnerable to deception.

Have you put together yet why it's so important to allow Jesus to clear away our old materials? Those judgments and lies we've internalized are vulnerable places where we don't know the difference between dirt and chocolate. For example, Satan whispers in your ear that fear protects you (fear is the mud), and if you've made the judgment that fear is good, and you'd better listen to it, you'll eat the enemy's deception, hook, line, and sinker. Ugh! What a nasty taste in your mouth.

But if you know the truth from Jesus—"There is no fear in love. But perfect love drives out fear" (I John 4:18)—you are no longer vulnerable to the judgment that fear is good or the lie that you need fear to protect you. You will walk in the freedom provided by Christ, knowing that whatever your circumstances, His love covers you, His arms hold you, and He walks with you through them all. As Scripture says, "Whoever dwells in the shelter of the Most High will rest in the shadow of the Almighty (Psalm 91:1).

So, let's take a look at our own structures we've built and see what materials need to be cleared out to make way for God's dwelling to be completed within us.

Consider This

1. In what ways have you seen Jesus at work in your life, calling you to Him, even before you accepted Him as your Savior?

2. What aspects of God's nature did He put into you at your creation? In other words, how do you reflect the character of God into the world?

3. What aspects of God's nature do you *not* have? (These are the parts of His nature that He must complete by joining with you to create a strong foundation for His internal dwelling.)

4. In what areas of your heart have you done a "deep dive" to explore with Jesus and gain insight? What did you discover there?

5. What areas in your heart need further exploration—to "dig down deep" with Him for further cleansing and healing?

6. If you were to "estimate the cost" of building your Kingdom dwelling, what are the things you will have to sacrifice? What needs to be blasted away by Jesus? What are you willing to give up to establish His dwelling within your heart?

7. How have you entered into a "covenant with death" and "made falsehood your hiding place"? In other words, what lies have you clung to as a refuge?

8. In what ways have you built "levels" into your internal structure, using hierarchical views of yourself in comparison to others? How have those levels influenced how you see and feel about yourself?

9. In what contexts have you seen fear as a good or helpful thing? What are your thoughts when you read "fear is different from wisdom"?

10. What evidence have you seen in your life that Christ has made you a "new creation"? What old has gone? What new has come?

11. How would you characterize your building materials you bring to the construction of your inner dwelling with Jesus? What materials do you believe are wood, hay, and straw? Which ones are gold, silver, and costly stones?

12. Which qualities do you have as one who inherits the Kingdom (for example, humility, righteousness, faith, sacrifice, a transformed heart, the fruit of the Spirit, love)? Which qualities do you need Jesus' help to receive?

13. Of the "innate materials" listed (exploration, adventure, purpose, creativity, imagination, connection, joy), which ones do

you freely express? Which ones have been repressed or controlled in your life?

14. Where have you allowed your freedom to be perverted into a justification for continuing to sin? Where have you allowed your freedom to be stolen from you in an attempt to maintain the illusion of control?

15. In what areas have you been deceived by the enemy in the past? In what ways has God begun the process of clearing away the "old materials" in your construction of your inner dwelling?

CHAPTER FOUR
DECONSTRUCTION, RECONSTRUCTION

One thing you need to know before we begin to explore the deconstruction of your internal structures: you have been made perfect.

I imagine a flurry of responses to this statement, like, "What?? You just pointed out how my materials are lacking. How can you turn around and say I've been made perfect?"

I'm not the one saying it. Hebrews 10:14 says it: "For by one sacrifice *he has made perfect forever* those who are being made holy." His sacrifice has made you perfect forever. Sin—all sin—has been absolved once and for all. "'Their sins and lawless acts I will remember no more.' And where these have been forgiven, sacrifice for sin is no longer necessary" (Hebrews 10:17-18).

It's important for you to accept that His sacrifice has accomplished your perfection. Now, I know you're probably looking at your many flaws and continued sin in your life, and saying, " *This* is perfect? No way!" But you're not discriminating between the spirit and the soul (heart and mind) in your assessment. Your spirit has been washed (I Corinthians 6:11), cleansed (II Peter 1:9), and made "whiter than snow" (Psalm 51:7). You have been clothed with Christ (Galatians 3:27). Your robes are made white in the blood of the Lamb (Revelation 7:14).

At the same time, the structures you have built over the course of your life still stand in your flesh and soul, influencing your behavior and thoughts—old neural pathways, old habits, and old beliefs. Yes, these structures must come down, but they are not to be sources of shame. Because your spirit is made perfect, "Therefore, there is now no condemnation for those who are in Christ Jesus" (Romans 8:1). No condemnation means no shame. As you give weight to your sin through feelings of shame, you undo what Jesus has done on the cross, which freed you from the shame of sin and made you perfect.

The interesting thing about shame is that it keeps you *bound* to the sin. You keep repeating the same mistakes over and over again. Instead of helping you repent (turn from the behavior), you get stuck in it like being trapped in a quagmire. Here is the internal logic: *if I'm a bad person (a sinner=a bad person), there's nothing I can do about that. I'm just bad. So, I can't help but be bad.* This line of reasoning leaves you believing you are powerless to choose differently and feeling trapped in your "badness" beyond your ability to walk a different road.

But if you truly know, deep in your heart, that you have *no shame* because you have been made perfect by the sacrifice of Jesus, once and for all, then you may freely approach the throne of grace with confidence (Hebrews 4:16), and with His help you can willingly make changes to your behavior by walking in accord with His Spirit (Galatians 5:16). Focusing on shame hinders what God desires and is still working on in you—to make you holy. (Note the second half of the Hebrews 10:14 verse—you are *being made holy*). You "are being transformed into His image with ever-increasing glory, which comes from the Lord, who is the Spirit" (II Corinthians 3:18).

That's why Jesus had to make us perfect before He could make us holy. As long as shame had a foothold in us, we were not free to walk out our transformation through His Spirit and work out our salvation with His help (Philippians 2:12). We wouldn't approach the throne of grace with confidence but with our eyes downcast and our faces turned away. Shame closed us off to His presence and shut down any movement into the new life He desires for us.

So, your spirit—which is unified with God (I Corinthians 6:17)— is perfected. You don't have to do one single thing to *be* perfect because He has *made* you perfect. Do you recall what I said about perfectionism being the enemy of self-valuing, and how the more we strive to be good enough, the more we're convinced we can never be good enough for God's love? God has removed this struggle for us. We don't have to strive for something we have been freely given already. Sin no longer taints your true nature. He remembers your sins no more. Shame has no more hold over you because sin has lost its power. Now, you are free to be made holy.

But what is holiness? To be holy means to be dedicated, consecrated (declared sacred), and set apart for God. Holiness assumes a *total* devotion to God. Nothing is held back. Nothing is clung to other than Jesus.

The journey to holiness is lifelong, a passage from the old self to the new, from the worldly self to the eternal life. Holiness means truly knowing who God is—His character, His nature, and His love—for you can't devote yourself to someone you don't know. It means shifting your focus off the values of the world and dedicating yourself to Kingdom ways. It means letting go of the Edenic lie of self as God, as well as all the other lie beliefs that go along with the flesh, and allowing Jesus to change your thoughts to truth and fill your heart with love. I've described being made holy as the deconstruction of your internal structures and the building of your inner Kingdom dwelling.

You can't approach the deconstruction of your inner structure from a place of shame. It simply won't work. You will remain bound to those structures and stuck with what you've built. Accepting the truth that you have been made perfect is the first, essential step of the deconstruction process.

The journey toward holiness continues all the way to your heavenly dwelling. How much of the journey you complete here determines how fully you live in the Kingdom of God now.

The Way of Holiness

Isaiah 35:8 & 9, talking about the coming Messiah, states, "And a highway will be there; it will be called the Way of Holiness; it will be for those who walk on that Way. The unclean will not journey on it; wicked fools will not go about on it. But only the redeemed will walk there." Our way of holiness is the narrow path—our journey toward our

Kingdom dwelling—walked in partnership with Jesus. Only those who walk in Kingdom ways will journey on this road.

Paul urges us not to be deceived—we can't unite ourselves with sin and remain united with Christ (Romans 6:9-11). The old structures are meant for demolition. They cannot remain connected with our perfected spirit. Knowing our spirits are made perfect by His sacrifice, we desire our souls and bodies to join with Jesus as well. Thus, we choose to make the journey on the Way of Holiness.

Before we can begin the journey, we must know who God is for ourselves. When we don't know God, we are "senseless children" without understanding (Jeremiah 4:22). It isn't enough to know *about* God from another's teaching. In fact, without personal knowledge, we can easily be taught false beliefs about God's nature and character, whether unknowingly or intentionally. That's why our relationship with Him is so important. Understanding through experience leads to wisdom. "No longer will they teach their neighbor, or say to one another, 'Know the LORD,' because they will all know me, from the least of them to the greatest" (Jeremiah 31:34).

We can also perceive God incorrectly when we judge Him through the lens of our lies. Our distorted views can color how we perceive God. For example, an experience of a distant, unloving father growing up can lead to an assumption that God is distant, "up there" somewhere uninvolved and uncaring. To prevent these distortions, we need a strong base in knowledge of Scripture to support our experiences of Him.

But it isn't enough to know God only from reading the Scriptures. We must know God intimately, through His presence in our hearts: "I will give them a heart to know me, that I am the LORD. They will be my people, and I will be their God, for they will return to me with all their heart" (Jeremiah 24:7). The best way to know anyone is through communication in relationship. Toward this purpose, God gives us prayer. Prayer was never intended to be a rote set of words we repeat or a series of request we throw up to God. Nor was prayer meant only for church or at the dinner table. Prayer is intimate, connected, and powerful when we open our hearts to experience God through genuine communication with Him.

Paul gives us a picture of the Way of Holiness in Romans 12. "Therefore, I urge you, brothers and sisters, in view of God's mercy, to offer your bodies as a living sacrifice, holy and pleasing to God—this is your true and proper worship. Do not conform to the pattern of this world, but be transformed by the renewing of your mind. Then you will be able to test and approve what God's will is—his good, pleasing and perfect will" (v. 1-2).

So once we know who God is, our journey to holiness begins with sacrifice—in imitation of Jesus—the living sacrifice of our bodies. "For we know that our old self was crucified with him so that the body ruled by sin might be done away with, that we should no longer be slaves to sin...In the same way, count yourselves dead to sin but alive to God in Christ Jesus. Therefore do not let sin reign in your mortal body so that you obey its evil desires. Do not offer any part of yourself to sin as an instrument of wickedness, but rather offer yourselves to God as those who have been brought from death to life; and offer every part of yourself to him as an instrument of righteousness" (Romans 6:6, 11-13).

And what is the sin of the flesh? Yes, it is the sin of Eden, the belief that we can be like God, knowing good and evil. Paul is calling us to allow Jesus to crucify our sin nature/flesh, "that we should no longer be slaves to sin" (v. 6). The first step on the Way of Holiness is to offer up the Edenic sin to God for destruction. It's a painful proposition, like a surgery to cut out an invasive cancer, but it's necessary. Otherwise, the cancer will reign in our mortal bodies and make us slaves to its desires.

Paul calls this sacrifice a true act of worship. By giving our bodies over to God, we *dedicate* our bodies to Him, and in doing so, we are set apart for God. This sacrificial act of worship begins the next part of the holiness process—our transformation by the renewing of our minds (12:2). As we are made new in our thinking, then we can know

God's will and follow Him in righteousness. Becoming "slaves" to righteousness leads to holiness (Romans 6:19).

How does righteousness appear in us? Let's look again to Romans 12 for the answers. First, Paul says we will think of ourselves with "sober judgment," not thinking hierarchically anymore, but recognizing that all of the people of God have different gifts and equal value (v. 3-8). Sincere love will be in evidence, of course, for how could we be unified with Christ and not love? (v. 9). This love will be devoted, honoring, and selfless in nature (v. 10), and without pride or conceit (v. 16).

We will hate evil (v. 9)—think about this one for a moment. Two kingdoms exist—two types of paths—one in the realm of evil (the wide, broad path) and one is the realm of God (the narrow way). Anything not of the Kingdom of God is of the realm of the enemy, and Paul is admonishing us to hate what is evil. In other words, he is instructing us to hate the lies, the deceptions, the influences to sin, the hatred, the violence, the division, and the destruction that is the enemy's realm. We are to shun and reject it, absolutely, but even beyond that, we are to *hate* the evil. Do you truly hate what is evil? Or has the enemy deceived you to think things of the enemy's realm are enjoyable, pleasurable, desirable, or acceptable?

We will also cling to what is good (v. 9). To cling to something has the connotation of gripping it tightly and never letting go, to latch onto it like someone drowning would hang onto a life preserver. As we walk in accord with His Spirit, we will hold tightly to Him (for He is the only One who is good) and allow Him to direct our paths (Psalm 119:35). This is what it means to walk the narrow way that leads to righteousness, and then holiness.

Paul also mentions spiritual zeal and fervor, painting quite a different picture from the stereotypical going to church on Sunday (for some, out of obligation) as your spiritual act of service. As we walk with the Lord toward holiness, we will gain an increasing passion for Jesus, such that talking to Him constantly (I Thessalonians 5:17 NET) will be as natural as breathing, and not talking to Him will result in an ache and a thirst in our souls that must be quenched. We'll want Him more than anything else in our lives. We will be genuinely dedicated and set apart for God.

The fruits of the Spirit will flow freely—joy in our certain hope, patience in our suffering, and faithfulness in our prayers (Romans 12:12). Doesn't it make sense that if we are walking in accord with the Spirit, His fruits will be in evidence? "A good tree is not able to bear bad fruit, nor a bad tree to bear good fruit" (Matthew 7:18). We will be recognized by our fruit (v. 20).

Generosity, hospitality, and harmony will also flow naturally from our walk with the Spirit toward holiness (v. 14-16). Jesus was clear in His instruction to give to the poor and help those in need (Mark 10:21, Luke 12:33, Luke 10:25-27). Although Jesus stated He came to bring division (Luke 12:51-53), He referenced separating the weeds from the wheat (Matthew 13:30)—good from evil. Those who follow Jesus are to live in harmony with one another (I Corinthians 1:10, 12:25), without divisions. We will also live at peace with everyone, even nonbelievers, to whatever extent we are able by our choice (v. 18). These instructions continue the focus on the outpouring of love and the fruits of the Spirit.

We will not respond to evil with evil, curse our persecutors, or take revenge on our enemies (v. 14, 17, 19). These actions, all very human, are all opposed to the fruit of love. I've observed how evil feeds evil—for example, when someone tries to control us, we often respond by escalating our control, or when someone is cruel to us, we often act in kind. I see spiritual warfare in these responses. The enemy stirs up certain attitudes in one person, and the negative spirit quickly infests others. If we are set apart for God, we will not feed on the negative, but will respond in love, grace, mercy, and kindness. We will see the other person as God sees them, not as their behavior colors our lenses. We will bless others, and not curse them by passing on any evil (v. 14, 21).

Finally, we will meet others where they are, just as Jesus meets us where we are and came to us so that we could know Him. If others are rejoicing, we will rejoice with them. If they are mourning, we will mourn with them (v. 15). The expression of empathy (coming alongside others in their feelings through shared understanding) is one of the strongest ways to create connection with people. The Spirit will foster empathy in our hearts, which will naturally connect us with others. Through that connection, we will be able to share the fruit of love in the way most likely to be received. As Paul explains, "Love is the fulfillment of the law" (Romans 13:10). In this way, we will be like Christ when we enter our heavenly dwelling (I John 3:2).

Counterintuitive Kingdom

Surrounding your perfected spirit stands a structure you've built over the years, a home—or more accurately, a prison—of your own design. This structure hinders your spirit's expression and keeps you locked away from the full experience of your relationship with Jesus. As a result, your body and soul take precedence over your spirit—first, the body (the flesh), then the soul (thoughts and emotions in your mind and heart).

But God's design was for your spirit to take precedence over the soul and body. Look at Adam and Eve. Their focus was on their communion with God, walking with Him in the garden. They weren't aware they were unclothed. They had no concern about what they would eat.

In fact, Jesus taught us to return to this state of being. "Therefore I tell you, do not worry about your life, what you will eat or drink; or about your body, what you will wear. Is not life more than food, and the body more than clothes? Look at the birds of the air; they do not sow or reap or store away in barns, and yet your heavenly Father feeds them. Are you not much more valuable than they?" (Matthew 6:25-26). God's original design didn't include fear or shame.

We didn't worry. We didn't feel the need to cover ourselves. We didn't have to hide. In Eden before the fall, the spirit had primacy over all.

As is often the case in the Kingdom of God, the worldly subverts the heavenly, so when we read about the Kingdom in Scripture, we see Jesus' descriptions as strange, backwards, and counterintuitive to what we think we know. For example, Jesus tells a story of workers in a vineyard. Some worked the whole day, while some worked only an hour, but all received the same wage. The day laborers complained, but the landowner pointed out that he paid them all what he agreed to pay them. By human standards this response seemed unfair, but in the Kingdom, it is just, because they received as they were promised (Luke 20:1-16).

When asked who is the greatest in the Kingdom of heaven, Jesus responded by calling a child over and saying, "Truly I tell you, unless you change and become like little children, you will never enter the kingdom of heaven. Therefore, whoever takes the lowly position of this child is the greatest in the kingdom of heaven" (Matthew 18:3-4). In this world, children are treated as lowly quite often. Certainly, they are not seen as the greatest. Those in lowly position in the world are often scorned and rejected or dismissed as insignificant. Yet, Jesus turns these ideas on their heads, calling children and those of lowly position "great."

The first will be last. The least is the greatest. Yes, Kingdom ideas are counterintuitive to worldly perspectives. The same is true for our internal states. We give preference to the body's wants over the spirit's desires. We give weight first to our feelings rather than listening and following the truth. We believe our own thoughts over the whispers of the Spirit in our spirit. To walk toward holiness, we must allow Jesus to turn our inner being right side-up, giving the spirit preeminence over the soul and body. He must restore us to our intended state.

Unfortunately, the rigid structures of your current "home" hold everything in place, like a steel cage that keeps your spirit trapped in bondage, stuck and unable to move freely or express openly. So, before your spirit can be set free and given primacy, your self-constructed structures must be demolished.

Out with the Old

Let's take a look, then, at the structures we build as our internal home/prison. Very early in our lives, we learn that sometimes the world isn't a safe place. To different degrees, whether it's by accident or intent, we get hurt. So, our first "room" we build is our "Panic Room"—a place where we can hide our spirits away from the pain and hurts of the world.

Before we build the Panic Room, we are out in the open, exposed for all to see, which is a beautiful thing. Our spirits dance and sing with abandon, we play without embarrassment, we speak without filters, and we love with all our hearts. But we don't stay open long. Perhaps someone teases us or laughs at us. Maybe an older sibling criticizes us, or a parent yells at us. Perhaps we fail at something we try, and we become our worst critic. The pressure begins early to cover up and hide ourselves. The enemy is quick to tell us we aren't safe while exposed.

But how do we interact with the world when we are hiding in our Panic Room? Our genuine selves can't. So, we construct a Formal Living Room and set up a façade—a false self— to greet those who want to engage with us. The façade is created based on the feedback we've received about what is acceptable and what is not in our true selves. The Formal Living Room gives the best first impression possible—or at least what we believe is a good impression. All may enter, but few get past the living room door.

Eventually, we figure out the Panic Room is only necessary when we are under duress, and the Formal Living Room isn't very comfortable to live in, so we construct a Hallway that leads to our Playroom (which converts to a Family Room as we get older). We use the Hallway as a kind of lookout post, a place where we peek out from the Panic Room to see if the coast is clear. We watch life happening from the Hallway, and when someone in the Formal Living Room appears safe, having passed whatever tests we've put in place, we may grant them entry into the Playroom/Family Room—that is, until they do or say something hurtful or that we perceive as dangerous, at which point they are ejected from the structure, and we retreat back to the Panic Room.

Someone with healthy relationships will allow ready access to the Playroom/Family Room. But before long, the Playroom/Family Room gets cluttered with stuff, and we become embarrassed for anyone to enter. That's when we construct our Basement. We stuff all the parts of ourselves we're ashamed of into the deep, dark Basement. Now, we have two hiding places—one that contains all our ugly secrets, where we go when we feel bad about ourselves (our shame room) and one with thick walls and impenetrable doors (our fear room).

When we get old enough to desire intimacy with others, we construct a Bedroom, but the nature of this room depends on our experiences in relationships to this point. If our relationships have been relatively healthy, our Bedroom will be a place where those people we want deepest relationships with may come and connect intimately with our true selves.

But if we've been abused or neglected by significant people in our lives, our Bedroom might more resemble a Panic Room than a place of intimacy. It will be well-defended, and most likely only one or two people will ever be admitted. Similarly, if we've been severely traumatized, it's likely our Bedroom will be closed to all except ourselves as a place of respite. In both of these cases, we may even construct a second faux-Bedroom where we admit people for a false connection through physical means, co-dependency, or objectification, but this so-called Bedroom is detached completely from the true self. Only the façade may enter.

All of these rooms are constructed on an incomplete foundation, which means they can crumble and fall at any time. The normal storms of life can topple the structure and leave a collapsed heap in their wake. And when that happens, we rebuild our structures with thicker walls and deeper basements, thinking these alterations will protect us. We don't understand that our broken foundation means our structure will not stand, no matter how many modifications we make. We also fail to realize that the more we live from the false self, the more disconnected we become from our real selves, until our true identity is hidden from us completely and never sees the light of day.

Another truth we don't realize as we build up our illusion of self-protection is that Jesus lives in *all our rooms*. Remember, He goes before us (John 14:2-3). So, as we scurry into our Panic Room in fear, He's there. When we skulk into our Basement in shame, He's there. We think our façade shields us, but He's there in our Formal Living Room, our Hallway, and our Playroom/Family Room. He knows us intimately already, more than we know ourselves. "Where can I go from your Spirit? Where can I flee from your presence? If I go up to the heavens, you are there; if I make my bed in the depths, you are there. If I say, 'Surely the darkness will hide me and the light become night around me,' even the darkness will not be dark to you; the night will shine like the day, for darkness is as light to you" (Psalm 139:7-8, 11-12).

Jesus is there, constantly at work demolishing your false structure. He uses whatever means at His disposal to accomplish His goal, which is your freedom. Let me repeat, *His work is for your freedom*. He begins with direct challenges to your belief you can be your own God. He brings His truth against the lie, He uses circumstances to challenge its veracity, and He will even use the enemy's tactics and turn them for good by illuminating the cracks in your foundation. What you perceive as suffering may in fact be Jesus tearing down your false structure, for whatever is intended for evil, God turns to accomplish good (Genesis 50:20).

So, how does His transformation take place? As I described, your early experiences laid in old neural pathways, connecting a set of your physical, emotional, perceptual, cognitive, and spiritual responses to those early events. When similar thoughts and emotions are stimulated in the present, you reexperience the flood of the original experience, along with all the other, similarly connected experiences you've had over the years.

Think of it as a well holding all your experiences connected to a particular set of responses. Each new experience throws a bucket down the well and pulls out all the old experiences in a flood. Then, the new experience is added back into the well. The neural pathways are reinforced with each reexperiencing.

For example, let's say you perceive your parent's divorce as a rejection of you by your father. This rejection carries a certain set of responses throughout your body and soul, which are laid into your brain as neural pathways. Each perceived rejection that follows, throughout your life, is connected to this original experience of rejection, and each new experiencing deepens your belief that you are worthy of rejection.

You may also have another perception based on this same experience, a second well of feelings and thoughts, such as a sense of not mattering enough to your parents for them to work out their issues or a belief that nothing in life is stable and secure. That "I don't matter" belief is reinforced each time someone dismisses you or treats you poorly. The sense of instability and insecurity is reinforced whenever anything bad happens. And on it goes.

Each "well" represents a different lie belief that must be deconstructed. Everyone believes lies, but your particular lie beliefs are based on your experiences and on what has been passed down from the generations before you. Yes, some of the lies you believe were taught to you because they are the lies your parents believe, and perhaps their parents before them. Lies are passed on like genetic material. One of the beautiful redemptions of God is the interruption of this lie transmission to the next generation. You can be the one to stop the cycle. But how?

Experience changes experience. In other words, neural pathways are rewritten when new experiences supersede the old. For new experiences to supplant old neural pathways, they must come from a greater authority or carry more weight because of the power of the experience. The problem, though, is what could possibly carry more weight than our first-learned experiences from our most significant caregivers? No present-day success, nothing another person could say, would ever surpass the weight we give to those first-learned experiences.

God's absolute authority is the key. His primary demolition tool is His deep, abiding love for you, the love described by Paul in Ephesians 3:18. His love is preeminent over all other experiences. It is vast, all-encompassing, unfailing, steadfast, never changing, and everlasting. By providing you with experiences of His love, He transforms your perceptions and understanding of your past experiences. He shows you His constant presence and displays His love for you in in the midst of them. He shares your pain and heartache. He carries you through them. And, most important of all, He offers you truth to alter your perceptions and interpretations of those early experiences. Because of His authority and the power of His love, He supersedes the old neural pathways and writes new ones.

However, your experience with God must be on all levels—a total experience of body, mind, emotion, and spirit, just like the original experience. It isn't enough to cognitively know about God or study Scripture enough to understand. I can believe Jesus loves me without truly *knowing* His love experientially. Transformation must occur in the whole of you.

Through prayer, invite Jesus to show you His presence in your past experiences. Ask for His truth to be made real to you in the midst of your lies. When a lie gets stirred up (your well is tapped), turn to Jesus in those moments and invite Him to intervene on your behalf. Ask Him what you need to see and know to be set free. Foster this type of conversational relationship with Jesus by talking to Him throughout the day, and pay attention when the still, small voice of God comes through. Open yourself up to see, sense, and/or hear Him in your whole being.

Don't be surprised or discouraged if you don't hear, see, or sense anything at first. Remember, you have an entire structure built from shame and fear vying to disconnect you from everyone, including Jesus. The enemy may try to interpret not hearing from Him as "Jesus doesn't care either" or "See, you aren't important" or "Jesus isn't real." Reject these beliefs and return to your prayer.

I believe, and my experience has proven it's true, that Jesus always has an entrance point, some way to breach our defenses and reach us. We may not know what that entrance point is or how to access it, but He does. *He goes before us.* So, be persistent and patient with yourself. He'll find a way to reach you if you are willing.

As you begin to experience Jesus' love in your spirit, soul and body, your perception of your early experiences begins to change. Instead of rejection, you *feel* loved. Instead of worthless, you *feel* valued. Instead of unstable and insecure, you *feel* protected. Through experiencing the depth of His love in the midst of all of your earliest experiences, you become more connected with Him until ultimately, you agree to the oneness He desires, and your spirit joined with His Spirit creates wholeness and completes your foundation.

In With the New

Division began in the garden with the knowledge of good and evil. Our belief that we can be like God divided us from God. Our fear and shame divided us from our true natures. The structure we built on that foundation divided us from others.

Until we allow our spirit to become one with His Spirit, we are not whole. But once He completes our foundation through unity with Him—accomplished through a deep experiencing of His love—we can reconnect with our true identity and express our created nature. Once our true self is set free and fully expressed, then we can reconnect with others in love.

With Jesus in unity with our spirit, our foundation is now secure and strong. We have "dug deep" and allowed Him to demolish our old, self-created foundation. From that secure foundation, Jesus begins the rebuilding process, the construction of our inner dwelling place with Him.

His floorplan begins with three pillars—Love, Freedom, and Faith—built on the firm foundation you and He have established. These pillars anchor your dwelling in its foundation and provide a structure for its design. From there, imagine an open, airy floorplan, filled with light, and a lush garden, abundant with fruit and flowers, whose fragrances flow freely throughout your dwelling.

He starts with the outer walls, which He builds from His truth and His transcendent peace. His truth combined with our faith acts as a shield, deflecting the attacks of the evil one and holding in place, like a belt, all of our other armor so that we may stand firm in the freedom He has provided (Ephesians 6:10-18). His peace acts as a guard over our hearts and minds, protecting us from worrying about our circumstances or allowing them to determine how we feel (Philippians 4:7).

These God-designed protections, unlike our self-protection, actually work. Truth doesn't change in the face of the winds of circumstance or the *hebel* of the world. Truth doesn't shift based on feelings or the opinions of others. Truth is stable and secure. So, in the face of all external forces, truth remains standing. We can always rely on His truth and can remain in it, shielded by it from all lies that would seek to derail us.

His peace, a peace beyond anything we can create, or the enemy can mimic, warns us about encroaching spiritual attacks. We can use it to discern the presence of evil. Anything that disrupts our peace, even a little, is not of God, so we can know to reject it, stand against it, and seek Jesus' help to defeat it. His peace, then, is an excellent barometer of our spiritual state of being.

Rather than going straight into a formal living room, Jesus constructs an Entrance Foyer at our front door. The Foyer allows the two of us to determine what or who is granted admittance. We stand in the Foyer and ask, "Who is it?" And Jesus tells us who or what to let in. Perversions or distortions of truth are not allowed. Evil is not allowed. Old, unhealthy behaviors, harmful patterns, and worldly ways are not admitted. The untrustworthy, the damaging, the abusive, the cruel, and the hate-filled are not allowed access to our hearts.

Once admitted through the Foyer, there's no need for a formal sitting area. Jesus' home goes straight into the Gathering Room. But unlike the Family Room, this room is open and welcoming, with high ceilings and plenty of space and windows. It is filled with genuineness and light. Our true selves live expansively and vulnerably within its truth and peace walls. Can you envision yourself, truly free and authentically you, sharing this space with Jesus and inviting others to join you?

The Gathering Room is open onto a kitchen area, where we can share meals and fellowship with others. The food we share is both physical and spiritual sustenance. There's no need for walls inside the dwelling because Jesus' walls of truth and peace are all the protection we need. There's no need for a Hallway or Panic Room or Basement because we have no fear or shame. Joy abounds, and love is freely shared with all who enter. The air is alive with the energy of connection and authenticity. We are seen and known, and we see those who join us here through Jesus' eyes.

One more room is added to our dwelling. Jesus calls it Sanctuary. It is our place of solitude and rest, where we commune with Him in the most complete intimacy we've ever known. This room is soft and warm and inviting. Music soothes our hearts and quiets our minds. There, the oneness we share with Jesus in our spirit is fully experienced in our soul. "Yes, my soul, find rest in God; my hope comes from him. Truly he is my rock and my salvation; he is my fortress, I will not be shaken. My salvation and my honor depend on God; he is my mighty rock, my refuge. Trust in him at all times, you people; pour out your hearts to him, for God is our refuge" (Psalm 62:5-8).

We have been made whole in this dwelling with Jesus. Division no longer plagues us. All of the factures and cracks in our foundation are healed. We are one with the Holy Spirit, free to approach the throne of grace with confidence. Our perfect spirit, our soul, and our body are reunified. Our true identity is free to pour out into others, and we are open to love God and receive God's love without barriers, protections, or defenses. The fruit of the Spirit adorns our dwelling, blossoming in us in abundance, and the love of God is a river of living water flowing from within us into the world.

Ours is an unpretentious home, beautiful in its simplicity and filled with character, hope, and love. The deconstruction process may be painful and heart-wrenching; the reconstruction process may be arduous, time-consuming, and challenging. But the final dwelling is worth any cost, for there, we find rest for our soul.

Our Heavenly Home

Our heavenly dwelling will be the fulfillment of what we sow in our inner dwelling. As Jesus said, "Truly I tell you, whatever you bind on earth will be bound in heaven, and whatever you loose on earth will be loosed in heaven" (Matthew 18:18). Is our food the food that spoils, or will it endure to eternal life? (John 6:27). What we store up as treasures will be manifest, whether those are worldly treasures that burn up in the fire or Kingdom treasures that enrich our dwelling in heaven.

Jesus teaches us, "Everyone will be salted with fire" (Mark 9:49). But what does He mean by this phrase, "salted with fire"? In Jesus' time, salt was used as a preservative and to purify meats, removing moisture, bacteria, and other impurities that could destroy the meat and render it inedible. Reading the verse in context, Jesus appears to be speaking of remaining in the Kingdom—both in the present and in the future—or stumbling into hell, which is separation from God—again, both hell in our present lives and eternal separation.

Jesus is saying that anything that causes you to feel distant or separated from Him needs to be addressed, swiftly and severely. We are to get rid of it, no matter what it takes. Listen to His words: "It is better for you to enter life maimed than with two hands to go into hell, where the fire never goes out. It is better for you to enter life crippled than to have two feet and be thrown into hell" (Mark 9:43, 45). Viewed through the lens of these verses, the process of tearing down the old structure and rebuilding the Kingdom home takes on a sense of urgency and eternal significance.

It is in this context that Jesus states everyone will be salted with fire. The question is, what type of fire? Will you be salted (purified) with the fire of the Holy Spirit? Or will you be salted (preserved) with the fire of hell "that never goes out" (Mark 9:43)? Jesus said, ""I have come to bring fire on the earth, and how I wish it were already kindled!" (Luke 12:49). Jesus kindled the refiner's fire (Malachi 3:2), and it burns even now. The foundation we have built our lives based upon is revealed with the fire of the Holy Spirit. Everything we have sown is shown for what it is. What does His refining fire reveal in you?

Some live their lives with a thirst for love, joy, and peace that remains unsatisfied, with the unfulfilled desire to be seen and truly known that burns their soul with emptiness and sears their hearts with despair. Their fire is the unquenchable fire that never goes out. Some live with their feet in two kingdoms, believing in the Kingdom of God while living with their old structures still firmly in place. The fire will burn up what they've sown, and they will enter "as one escaping through the flames" (I Corinthians 3:15).

Then, there are those, like Mary, who have "chosen what is better" (Luke 10:42). They sit at the Lord's feet and listen to His words. They fix their eyes on what is eternal instead of focusing on the temporary offerings of the world (II Corinthians 4:18). They sow in love, to be reaped in the glorification of that sowing (Galatians 6:8, James 3:18). They live life now like they want to live life eternally.

Ecclesiastes teaches us about living for the transient and temporary, calling it "a chasing after the wind" (1:14). Ecclesiastes also says, "He has made everything beautiful in its time. He has also set eternity in the human heart" (3:11). You are made beautiful by Christ, perfect in your spirit and in the process of being made holy in your soul. You hold the eternal in your heart. If you join with Jesus to tear down the building of your design and reconstruct your Kingdom dwelling now, "the benefit you reap leads to holiness, and the result is eternal life" (Romans 6:22).

Revelation 21 uses imagery to attempt to give us a glimpse into our heavenly home. Visions of a place with no tears or mourning or death, and with no sea (symbolic for no sin); of a bride beautifully arrayed, and a city that shines with the glory of God, precious jewels, pure gold, and pearls coming down from heaven; of a mountain great and high; of a place whose light is the glory of God, so there is no night, and its gates are never shut—these images paint a picture of unimaginable beauty and majesty and glory and honor. It's beyond our ability to comprehend; yet, I imagine it barely brushes the edges of what we will behold when we arrive.

I asked Jesus to show me my heavenly dwelling, the one He has prepared for me. He gave me an image of a small log cabin nestled among thick, green trees, sitting on the side of a grassy hill. It's single story, but the front is covered in windows. The grass is a vibrant color of green I've only seen once—on a trip we made to New Zealand. At the base of the hill runs a lively stream. I can hear the rushing water from inside my cabin, which is lovely. But I spend most of my time outside, sitting at the base of the hill with my feet in the dancing water. Jesus sits beside me. We gaze together at the beauty of the mountain range before us, at the white clouds drifting across the crystalline blue sky, and at each other.

It's the most glorious thing I've ever seen. And it's perfect for me.

Ask Jesus to show you an image of your heavenly dwelling. Try not to impose your own ideas of what you might imagine; instead, be open to whatever He brings to mind. You'll recognize it when it comes to you. You'll feel drawn to it. You'll understand exactly why He made it the way He did, in ways no one else will comprehend. Your dwelling is one-of-a-kind.

In the meantime, we don't have to wait for His Kingdom to come. It's already here. It lives inside us because He lives within our hearts. So, let's talk about what it means to live in the Kingdom now and how to let the Kingdom flow from you into the world, for that is our purpose as Christians—to bring His Kingdom, visibly and perceptibly, and pour it into those around us.

Consider This

1. What is your response to this phrase: "you have been made perfect"?

2. What are some examples where shame has kept you bound to sin, repeating the same behaviors instead of turning from them?

3. What are your thoughts on my definition of holiness as being dedicated, consecrated, and set apart for God? In what ways are you living in holiness? In what areas does Jesus need to help you be made holy?

4. How would you answer if someone asked you, "Who is God?" (Don't offer a superficial response but use this question as an opportunity to really explore how you see God. What is His nature? What is His character?)

5. In what ways has God experientially revealed Himself to you? How have your lie beliefs distorted your view of God?

6. God asks that we "offer our bodies as a living sacrifice, holy and pleasing to God." How have you offered yourself as a sacrifice to God? What are some things you hold in your heart still that you need to offer as a sacrifice?

7. Holiness is described as seeing yourself in "sober judgment" without viewing yourself higher or lower than others or others higher or lower than you. In what areas do you see yourself with the eyes of sober judgment and others with the eyes of love?

8. What is your response to the admonition to hate evil? In what ways have you given evil a "pass" and allowed it to enter instead of taking a stand against it? What does it mean to you to "cling to what is good"? In what ways have you met evil with evil?

9. How would you assess your spiritual fervor and zeal? Where in your life do you see evidence of the free flow of the fruits of the Spirit?

10. Have you had the experience of someone meeting you where you are (mourning when you mourn, rejoicing when you rejoice)? How did that feel? Have you met someone where they are before? What was that like for you?

11. In what ways has your spirit-soul-body connection been inverted, such that your body and soul dominate the expression of your spirit? How does it feel when your spirit has dominion over your soul and body?

12. I offered detailed descriptions of the type of old structures we build in our self-designed internal home. Which ones do you see in evidence in your heart? Which descriptions were relatable to you? Which ones have already been torn down, and which remain to be demolished?

13. How do you respond to the phrase, "experience changes experience"? Where have you see this premised evidenced in your life?

14. I offered detailed descriptions of our internal Kingdom dwelling. Which ones do you see in evidence in your heart? Which descriptions were relatable to you? Which ones remain to be constructed? In what areas of your life are you still plagued by division?

15. When you ask Jesus to show you your heavenly dwelling, what do you see and experience?

CHAPTER FIVE

KINGDOM LIFE

Jesus did not come into this world to adapt Himself to the attitudes and viewpoints of this world. He came into this world to change the world, and He calls us to the same mission. As we live the Kingdom life and allow its fruit to flow freely from us into the world, we usher the Kingdom into our sphere and reclaim some of the ground lost to the evil one in Eden.

Jesus said He came to bring life "abundantly" (John 10:10 NET). He also said, "The Spirit gives life; the flesh counts for nothing. The words I have spoken to you—they are full of the Spirit and life" (John 6:63). In the Kingdom life, we don't measure the abundance of our life by the pleasure of our flesh or the standards of the world. The abundant Kingdom life is filled with the Spirit and truth (John 4:24). Jesus promised the Spirit lives with us and will be in us (John 14:17), His presence in us will be our source of truth (John 16:13), and the truth will make us free (John 8:32).

We are welcomed into the Kingdom life when we believe (John 3:16) and have faith (Romans 3:22) in Jesus. Our eternal life begins at that moment. When we willingly accept Jesus' sacrifice as our salvation (Romans 3:25), receive Him (John 1:12), and are sealed with the Holy Spirit within us (Ephesians 1:13), we are given the right to become children of God and citizens of His Kingdom. Living as citizens of the Kingdom means an upheaval of all we've known. Remember, "if anyone is in Christ, the new creation has come. The old has gone; the new is here!" (II Corinthians 5:17).

Intuitively, we would expect the first to be first, right? But in the Kingdom, the first is last, and the last is first (Matthew 20:16). We would expect the rich and powerful to have the best in life, but in the Kingdom, the poor are blessed (Luke 6:20). Hating our enemies just makes sense, right? They are, after all, our enemies. But in the Kingdom life, we love our enemies and pray for them (Matthew 5:43-44). To save our lives, we are told we must lose our lives (Matthew 16:25). What?

In fact, everything in the Kingdom life will be counterintuitive to what we expect. It won't make sense when stacked up against our prior perspectives. "For the message of the cross is foolishness to those who are perishing, but to us who are being saved it is the power of God" (I Corinthians 1:18); and "The person without the Spirit does not accept the things that come from the Spirit of God but considers them foolishness, and cannot understand them because they are discerned only through the Spirit" (I Corinthians 2:14). Because the Kingdom doesn't make sense without the Spirit, Jesus described the Kingdom life in parables, and those who had ears to hear received (Mark 4:9).

The Kingdom Key

Let's see what we can glean about living the Kingdom life from studying Jesus' parables. Jesus tells us that one parable contains the secret to understanding the Kingdom of God: The Parable of the Sower (Mark 4:1-20). This parable is like a key for unlocking our understanding of the Kingdom of God and the rest of Jesus' parables.

The parable is divided into three parts: the parable itself, Jesus' commentary on the secret of the Kingdom, and His explanation of the parable. Jesus uses the analogy of planting because people at that time would've readily understood how planting seeds works and the amount of tending it takes to produce fruit. He begins with the parable, then let's the disciples know the secret of the Kingdom of God has been revealed to them, but to anyone "outside" the secret will be couched in parables.

Another significant element to notice is Mark quotes directly a verse from Isaiah here (6:9-10), which is something Mark does not do often. The fact that he quotes these verses here indicates the significance of this parable in understanding the Kingdom. According to Jesus, the Kingdom of God is a secret that must be revealed to us. We cannot perceive it or understand it as long as we are "outside" the kingdom.

The secret of the Kingdom of God is understood against the backdrop of Jesus' person. Who is He? In Him, the Kingdom of God has come into the world. Knowing Jesus is how we come to understand and experience the Kingdom of God.

The sower is Jesus. He came to sow seed. The seed He sows is the word (*logos,* translated here as the word). Jesus isn't referring here to the Bible. The Greek word, *logos,* refers to the transcendent, perfect, universal divine reason; the eternal and unchanging truth present from the beginning of creation. We know in John 1:1, *logos* was from the beginning, was with God, and was God. In John 1:14, we hear *logos* was made flesh and made His dwelling among us. Jesus' person is the *Logos,* the transcending, unifying, eternal, and unchanging truth. So, the seed He sows is Himself.

Jesus explains His seed is sown within four different kinds of hearts. The first heart He calls the path. In this heart, Jesus lands on it but the enemy (represented in the parable by birds) immediately comes and snatches it away. I would describe this heart as shut down, set in its ways, and perhaps holding onto the old rather than accepting the new. This heart may be unwilling to transform for Jesus, trying instead to fit Him into their preexisting paradigms.

The second heart He calls rocky ground. Jesus describes this heart as receiving Jesus with joy, but He doesn't take root, so when trouble or persecution comes, they wither and fall away. This type of heart might be shallow, fear-based, inflexible, and self-protected. You might experience someone with this kind of heart as having walls up. They might refuse to take risks or be vulnerable and exposed. This heart would be what Ezekiel 36:26 refers to as a "heart of stone."

Jesus describes the third heart is as filled with thorns or weeds. In this heart, other things choke out Jesus, and His presence produces no fruit. This heart is filled with lies, focused on self and selfish desires. This individual would be worldly in their understanding, self-seeking and self-gratifying. Lacking humility, they might approach Jesus for what they think He can do for them, but their motive is not one of love.

The fourth heart is good soil. Jesus explains this heart very simply: they hear and receive Jesus. Then, the heart bears great fruit in varying amounts because of receiving Jesus. This heart would be open, willing, softened, flexible, and holding nothing back from full commitment to Jesus and the relationship and partnership with Him.

According to this key parable, the secret of the Kingdom is this: the Kingdom is found in the heart. Jesus comes to you to unite you with God by offering Himself to your heart. Those inside the Kingdom are those who receive Him and bear fruit.

Our hearts can at any time become a hardened path, rocky ground, or weed-choked. We need to tend our hearts, much like a planter tends his fields, and we need to nurture the seed sown so the enemy doesn't snatch Jesus away, times of difficulty don't wither our connection with Him so we fall away, or weeds don't choke Him out and fill His place in our hearts.

Jesus has come to reveal the hidden things (Mark 4:22), if we are willing to listen. The Kingdom of God was hidden from us; now it has been brought to light. But the warning in the parable is to listen with care. According to Jesus, if we don't understand this parable, we won't understand any of His parables (Mark 4:13).

Paul's further application of the Parable of the Sower is, "Whoever sows to please their flesh, from the flesh will reap destruction; whoever sows to please the Spirit, from the Spirit will reap eternal life" (Galatians 6:8). Our worldly perspective would tell us sowing for ourselves will reap benefit for ourselves. But in the counterintuitive Kingdom of God, sowing for the flesh/sin nature of trying to be our own God brings only destruction, but sowing to please God instead of ourselves reaps the Kingdom life.

Jesus continues using the analogy of seeds in the parables the Growing Seed and the Mustard Seed (Mark 4:26-29, 30-33). In the Growing Seed parable, Jesus explains how the soil produces a crop from the seed on its own, without knowing how the growth is happening. Jesus is talking here about the process of growth, both the growth of the Kingdom within us and the spread of the Kingdom into the world. Jesus spreads the seed of His presence within us, and without us knowing how, the seed grows and produces a good crop. The seed grows roots in us first, then reaches up to the light, then develops, then comes to full fruit and is harvested when ripe.

You recall from the Parable of the Sower how seeds planted in good soil in our hearts produce fruit. Here, Jesus goes further to explain how the fruit or crop within us is produced, not based on our efforts or work but based solely on the quality of the seed and the soil. We don't know how the growth takes place exactly; we just receive the fruit of that growth.

Paul expands on the analogy, speaking of the seed dying so the new plant can grow: "What you sow will not come to life unless it dies. And what you sow is not the body that is to be, but a bare seed—perhaps of wheat or something else. But God gives it a body just as he planned, and to each of the seeds a body of its own. It is the same with the resurrection of the dead. What is sown is perishable, what is raised is imperishable" (I Corinthians 15:36-38, 42 NET). Just as the parable speaks of our growth and transformation into living in the Kingdom of God through His Spirit planted in the soil of our hearts, Paul talks about beginning as a natural body and being raised a spiritual body, sown perishable and raised imperishable. We are sown in death and resurrected to Kingdom life where we "bear the image of the man of heaven" (v. 49), who is Jesus. This is the Kingdom of God within us.

Reclaiming the world for the Kingdom also grows in this way. Through Christ within us, we sow seeds in others. We don't know, and may never know in this world, what those seeds are doing in the hearts of those in whom we've sown. But every seed has the potential to grow into a mature plant, spreading its own seeds, and through this process, the Kingdom is ushered into the world—the harvest of the parable.

In the Mustard Seed parable, Jesus is comparing the Kingdom of God to another type of seed, the smallest of all seeds. Jesus began His ministry very small, with just a few select followers, but then grew beyond all expectation. A mustard seed doesn't grow to be the largest of all garden plants with large branches naturally. Yet, in the parable, it grew so large that the birds could nest in its branches. In the same way, the seeds start small in our hearts, with basic truths and infant-like belief, but they grow and expand until they reach beyond any natural expectation for growth and transformational change.

But there is a warning in the parable as well, in the form of the birds nesting in the large branches. Some interpret this verse as meaning there is room in the Kingdom for the Gentiles to be a part of it and rest in it. Some say the birds mean anyone who is faithful can rest in the Kingdom. I don't agree with either of these interpretations, primarily because this parable is told in the context of the Parable of the Sower, which Jesus identifies as containing the secret to understanding all other parables of the Kingdom.

In the Parable of the Sower, the birds represent the enemy who comes and "snatches away" what is sown. In other words, they interfere with the heart receiving and understanding who Jesus is. They interfere with the oneness Jesus wants to establish with us. So, since these parables are presented as a unit, they are connected, their messages are connected, and their symbols are connected. The birds of the air represent the possibility of an interfering evil presence within the body of Christ. The parable warns that when the body grows large, there will be room for evil to set up shop—to nestle in and find a home in its shade.

If we examine how those taught by Paul strayed from his teachings, we can see evidence of what this parable is describing. For example, Paul described the downfall of the Galatians as a spell cast on them. "You foolish Galatians! Who has cast a spell on you? Before your eyes Jesus Christ was vividly portrayed as crucified! The only thing I want to learn from you is this: Did you receive the Spirit by doing the works of the law or by believing what you heard? Are you so foolish? Although you began with the Spirit, are you now trying to finish by human effort?" (Galatians 3:1-3 NET).

Paul's warning to us is the temptation to return to reliance on our own effort (the sin of Eden) is strong in us. The "birds" came into the body of Christ in Galatia and began to "distort the gospel of Christ" (Galatians 1:7) and sway them to return to justification by the law. This distortion happened quickly, too. Imagine how much the enemy may have distorted our views of Scripture and Jesus' teaching, given the length of time since His resurrection.

The Kingdom of God was hidden before Jesus came, but now it is here and present within us, and He has opened it to us to see and hear and understand. Now that we hold the key to understanding the Kingdom, let's explore the rest of Jesus' parables to see what else we might glean.

Beyond the Parable of the Sower and accompanying seed parables, which contain elements of all of the different types of parables, Jesus' parables fall loosely into four basic categories (with significant cross-over): parables on the division between the Kingdom of God and the realm of evil, parables about the coming of Christ, parables challenging the religious leaders and Jewish people, and parables describing the ways of the Kingdom. Some contain warnings; others offer instruction; still others challenge our old ways of thinking and living. Each one reveals crucial understandings of the Kingdom life if we have ears to hear.

Divided Kingdoms

We begin with the clear understanding that there is nothing in common between the Kingdom of God and the realm of the enemy, and nothing in common between Jesus and Satan (II Corinthians 6:15). In the same way, there is nothing in common between someone living the Kingdom life and someone living in the worldly realm—life in the Spirit vs. life in the flesh.

In response to the Pharisees' claim that Jesus drove out demons by the power of Satan, Jesus said, "Every kingdom divided against itself will be ruined, and every city or household divided against itself will not stand. If Satan drives out Satan, he is divided against himself. How then can his kingdom stand?" (Matthew 12:25-26). He goes on to explain, "But if it is by the Spirit of God that I drive out demons, then the kingdom of God has come upon you" (v. 28). In this statement, Jesus makes clear that the realm of the enemy is divided from the Kingdom of God.

Jesus follows up with two brief parables. The first presents His plans to deal with the enemy: "how can anyone enter a strong man's house and carry off his possessions unless he first ties up the strong man? Then he can plunder his house" (v. 29). Jesus has come to the world, the "strong man's house", to plunder—steal back—His children. To do so, He must first bind the strong man. In the second parable, He further demonstrates the clear division between good and evil. "Make a tree good and its fruit will be good, or make a tree bad and its fruit will be bad, for a tree is recognized by its fruit" (v. 33).

Similarly, Hebrews 4:12 describes how Jesus is a dividing sword, piercing into the attitudes of the heart. "For the word (*logos*) of God is alive and active. Sharper than any double-edged sword, it penetrates even to dividing soul and spirit, joints and marrow; it judges the thoughts and attitudes of the heart." Note once again the Greek word, *logos*, which refers to the transcendent, perfect, divine reason and truth, the *Logos* made flesh who dwells among us. Jesus divides truth from lie, soul from spirit, and good from evil. Of His purpose, He said, "I did not come to bring peace, but a sword" (Matthew10:34).

Two more parables depict the workings of the realm of evil. One story speaks to evil's attempts to infuse into the "bread" of our lives. "The kingdom of heaven is like yeast that a woman took and mixed into about sixty pounds of flour until it worked all through the dough" (Matthew 13:33). Yeast in Scripture represents sin or evil, so this parable is revealing the enemy's strategy of mixing in with the good to try to taint it. He accomplishes this goal in us by planting lies and continuing to reinforce them throughout our lives, as long as we allow it.

The other story goes like this: "The kingdom of heaven is like a man who sowed good seed in his field. But while everyone was sleeping, his enemy came and sowed weeds among the wheat, and went away. When the wheat sprouted and formed heads, then the weeds also appeared. The owner's servants came to him and said, 'Sir, didn't you sow good seed in your field? Where then did the weeds come from?' 'An enemy did this,' he replied. The servants asked him, 'Do you want us to go and pull them up?' 'No,' he answered, 'because while you are pulling the weeds, you may uproot the wheat with them. Let both grow together until the harvest. At that time I will tell the harvesters: First collect the weeds and tie them in bundles to be burned; then gather the wheat and bring it into my barn'" (v. 24-30).

Do you see the connection between the Mustard Seed parable and these parables? In the same way the birds nested in the branches, the woman mixes yeast in the dough and the man's enemy sows weeds among the wheat in his field. Taken together, these parables show how the Kingdom of God remains divided from the evil one's realm and can be recognized by the fruit produced, and how the enemy tries to infiltrate the Kingdom and must be separated by Jesus' sword of truth. They are parables of both division and discernment.

So, the Kingdom of God is like a field cleaved in half by the sword of truth. On one side, all things belonging to the enemy's realm exist. On the other are the things of the Kingdom. The two have no commonalities. They do not intersect. In the Kingdom, the enemy is not welcome. Jesus acts as the sword dividing good from evil. In the world, the enemy still grows alongside the children of God. Satan may try to "mix" himself into our lives, but a Kingdom life discerns through the Spirit and rejects his lies.

The End of the Age

The Parable of the Weeds and Wheat also addresses another topic that Jesus explained through parables, the coming of the "end of the age." According to Jesus' explanation of the parable's meaning, "The one who sowed the good seed is the Son of Man. The field is the world, and the good seed stands for the people of the kingdom. The weeds are the people of the evil one, and the enemy who sows them is the devil. The harvest is the end of the age, and the harvesters are angels. As the weeds are pulled up and burned in the fire, so it will be at the end of the age" (v. 37-40).

The way the plants grew together made it impossible to pull out the weeds without damaging the wheat. So, rather than try to pull the weeds, when harvest time comes, Jesus says the weeds will be collected and burned, and the wheat will be brought into the barn. The ultimate and absolute division between the two kingdoms will come with Jesus' return; however, within our hearts, the separation can already be happening, if we permit Jesus to excise the enemy's lies and schemes from us with His sword of truth.

The Parable of the Net (v. 47-50) contains the same message about the "end of the age." All fish collected in His net will be separated, the good fish into baskets, and the bad fish thrown away. The Parable of the Budding Fig Tree (Matthew 24:32-35) reminds us that, just as we know the change of seasons by looking at the signs in nature, we will know when Jesus' return is near by the signs He outlined in v. 6-31. Mark 13:34-37 and Matthew 24:45-51 speak about the importance of being watchful and prepared for the Master's return, but my favorite parable about watching for Jesus' return is the Parable of the Ten Virgins, because of what it teaches about *how* to prepare and be ready for His coming.

In Matthew 24:33-34, Jesus tells His followers: "Even so, when you see all these things, you know that it is near, right at the door. Truly I tell you, this generation will certainly not pass away until all these things have happened." Jesus is letting the disciples know they will have their own experiences of being hated because of Jesus, of being persecuted and turned over to death, of having false prophets claiming to be the Christ and false teachers misleading many—and as He said, all of those things happened before that generation passed away. Still, it was not the "end of the age."

In Scripture, prophesy often refers to more than one time period simultaneously. We've seen how Jesus' teaching to the disciples referred to events coming during their lifetime. Prophesy also speaks to an ultimate culminating event in a future time, in this case Jesus' return. "As lightning that comes from the east is visible even in the west, so will be the coming of the Son of Man" (v. 27). Other parables described the events that will happen when He comes, namely the separation of the weeds from the wheat and the good fish from the bad.

Prophesy is also applicable on a personal, individual level, describing what takes place in our hearts. We each experience our own gathering to Him at our death, which is our personal "end of the age." I also believe the Ten Virgins has something profound to say about the Kingdom of God in our hearts.

Having set the stage in Matthew 24, Jesus begins by describing what the Kingdom of Heaven will be like "at that time" (Matthew 25:1), meaning at the time the disciples would experience after His death and resurrection, at the end of the age, and during times of personal trial. The parable introduces ten virgins who are waiting for the bridegroom to come. Five of the virgins, described as "foolish" (v. 2), had lamps but didn't take extra oil with them to fill their lamps, but the five wise virgins "took oil in jars along with their lamps" (v. 4).

The bridegroom took much longer than they expected, and all of them feel asleep. At long last, when the midnight cry came that the bridegroom was coming, the foolish virgins asked to share the oil brought by the wise ones, because their lamps were going out. But the wise virgins pointed out they didn't have enough oil for both lamps and told the foolish ones to go buy their own oil.

Now comes the sad part of the story. "But while they were on their way to buy the oil, the bridegroom arrived. The virgins who were ready went in with him to the wedding banquet. And the door was shut. Later the others also came. 'Lord, Lord,' they said, 'open the door for us!' But he replied, 'Truly I tell you, I don't know you'" (v. 10-12). Jesus reiterated at the end of the parable to keep watch, "because you do not know the day or the hour" (v. 13).

The oil for their lamps refers to the presence of the Holy Spirit, providing light in the darkness. The lamps refer to our hearts, where the light of life resides. The wedding banquet refers to the Kingdom of God, which is within us now, is where we will go at our death, and is coming when Jesus returns, restoring God's original design.

The five wise virgins brought the Spirit of the Living God with them to fill their "lamps" and light their way through their darkness or time of difficulty. As they waited for the bridegroom to come, they focused on the infilling presence of the Holy Spirit as the thing of primary importance. They invested their resources wisely into that relationship, instead of spending their time, energy, and resources on other things. They prepared in advance instead of waiting until the last minute or ignoring the need for preparation. Whatever worldly things tried to distract them from their focus, they ignored. They were ready when midnight, the time of deepest darkness, came.

The five foolish virgins, however, brought their lamps but failed to invest in the oil, the intimate presence of the Holy Spirit, to fill their lamp. They knew about the bridegroom. They knew He was coming; yet, they didn't focus on preparing for His arrival or build that strength of relationship needed to sustain them through difficult times. When the time came, they ran out of oil.

Notice that all ten virgins fell asleep. I'm reminded of the disciples who couldn't stay awake with Jesus at Gethsemane. I believe this is an often ignored but important part of this story. Jesus is telling us that, no matter how deeply we love Him, we still succumb to the weakness of our flesh and "doze off" when things are smooth in our lives. Then, suddenly, the alarm is sounding, and the darkness is upon us. The question of the parable is, are we prepared?

Another important point is the bridegroom took a long time coming and arrived at midnight, the very last hour. We can't fail to prepare or be watchful for His coming, whether at the end of our physical lives or at the end of the age, simply because it's been a long time. We don't need to assume we've got plenty of time and plenty of oil.

Notice that the preparations of the five wise virgins cannot provide for the five foolish virgins. In other words, the Holy Spirit indwells and provides for me but can't sustain anyone else through their trials. We can't rely on someone else's relationship with God to carry us. Jesus is giving us an important warning here: prepare by investing in your relationship with God as of first importance, for when your time of trial, the end of your physical life, or the end of the age comes, you will not be able to stand in the light without the Holy Spirit's presence to sustain you.

The trials of the end of the age, according to Jesus, are unequaled (Matthew 24:21). At times of great trial or at the end of the age, the strong, overshadowing presence of the enemy and the distractions of emotions and pain in those times will make it difficult to "make it back in time" to be with the bridegroom in His Kingdom. If we go out seeking to purchase oil for our lamps, the nature of the times means the way may be blocked and the door closed.

The warning from Jesus is clear. We can't serve two masters. "Either you will hate the one and love the other, or you will be devoted to the one and despise the other" (Matthew 6:24). Let me repeat something we discussed earlier—we can't stand with one foot in the Kingdom and the other in the world, nor can we focus on our relationship with Jesus as our first priority while focusing on things of the world as equally important.

Whatever the foolish virgins were doing with their resources, they weren't investing in the presence of the Holy Spirit to give them light and truth. They were counting on what they had already to see them through to the end. It wasn't enough. The trial will come, and like the foolish virgins, if we don't already have that connected, intimate presence to hold us fast, we will lose our grip on the Kingdom and we will fall.

The Parable of the Bags of Gold (Matthew 25:14-30) has a similar message—watch and prepare for the return of the Master—but it includes an important addition about knowing the Master's nature and not being deceived about who He is. In the parable, three servants are entrusted—a key word—with their Master's wealth. The first two servants valued the trust the Master placed in them, and they responded by investing totally in the task, earning a great return on their gold. When the Master returned, He praised the two servants and invited them to share in His happiness.

The third servant, however, believed the Master to be "a hard man, harvesting where you have not sown and gathering where you have not scattered seed" (v. 24), so in fear, he hid the gold, and when the Master returned, the servant had nothing to show for the Master's trust. The Master's response was to take the gold away from the "wicked, lazy servant" (v. 26) and give it to the first servant, "For whoever has will be given more, and they will have an abundance. Whoever does not have, even what they have will be taken from them" (v. 29).

When we don't know God's true nature or recognize the great value of our relationship with Jesus—when we see a harsh taskmaster instead of a loving husband—we hide ourselves from God, like Adam and Eve in Eden after the fall. We bury the relationship out of fear of punishment. We don't invest our whole selves in our relationship with Jesus. We don't believe He would care about us or be involved in our everyday lives, and that leaves the burden squarely on us.

In a similar teaching, Jesus points out that we don't "bring in a lamp to put it under a bowl or a bed" (Mark 4:21-25). No, the light of our true nature is to be displayed openly to provide light for others, so they can see the Kingdom of God. Jesus' warning in this parable is, "With the measure you use, it will be measured to you—and even more. Whoever has will be given more; whoever does not have, even what they have will be taken from them" (v. 24-25). Like the wicked, lazy servant, when we hide the light of our identity, the great gift God entrusted to us, what we have will be lost.

We want to do well, to choose good things, to get it right—like the Pharisees did in their rigid attempt to follow the letter of the Law—but we can't without the presence of the Holy Spirit to guide us in the experience through an active relationship. Our choices made apart from God are fruitless. Of course, a relationship buried does not and cannot grow. Thus, even what we have is taken away by our fear, and it's our own belief about who God is that precludes the relationship He desires to have with us. We miss the truth that He has *entrusted* us with His love.

So, the Kingdom of God is like an infant, who loves with its whole being and gives trust without question or hesitation. Those who see the infant's true nature respond in kind, multiplying the love and trust and reaping a great reward. But those who put value in other things—whose heart is divided in loyalty and whose love is spread indiscriminately—and those who don't see the infant's true nature and allow fear of rejection and judgment to close their hearts end up separated from the infant, lost and alone.

The Kingdom embraces those who receive, value, and share in the love and the great trust that has been given as a gift to them. All others remain outside, where they have chosen to be.

Challenges

Several parables offer challenges to those who were missing or misconstruing the Kingdom of God. These parables ask questions about justice, doing God's will, faith, righteousness, and the consequences of rejecting the Kingdom of God.

The Pharisees, often the object of Jesus' most challenging parables, were rigid followers of the law, but more than that, they held to the traditions passed down from the elders—voluminous oral interpretations of the law. In many cases, the traditions were given more weight that the original law of Moses. These traditions added tremendous burdens on the people and excluded many from the Kingdom who couldn't follow the intricacies or expense of the traditions.

Jesus' harshest criticism fell on the Pharisees' applications of the law through the traditions of the elders. He said such things as, "You shut the door of the kingdom of heaven in people's faces. You yourselves do not enter, nor will you let those enter who are trying to" (Matthew 23:13), and "you have neglected the more important matters of the law—justice, mercy and faithfulness" (v. 23), and "You clean the outside of the cup and dish, but inside they are full of greed and self-indulgence" (v. 25).

Jesus made a statement that offended the Pharisees (Matthew 15:12), saying, "You hypocrites! Isaiah was right when he prophesied about you: 'These people honor me with their lips, but their hearts are far from me. They worship me in vain; their teachings are merely human rules.' Jesus called the crowd to him and said, 'Listen and understand. What goes into someone's mouth does not defile them, but what comes out of their mouth, that is what defiles them'" (Matthew 15:7-11).

You can understand, right? Quoting the Scriptures which the Pharisees held in such esteem against them would've been a great offense. Jesus is pointing out their elevation of the traditions over the law. He went on to challenge their interpretations of the law by focusing on the heart over the purity requirements. "For out of the heart come evil thoughts—these are what defile a person" (v. 19, 20).

Jesus told a parable making a similar point, the Parable of the Good Samaritan (Luke 10:29-37). A man was beaten by robbers and left for dead. Both a priest and a Levite "passed by on the other side" (v. 31) and left the man for dead. According to the traditions of the elders, to allow even their shadow to touch the bloody, unclean man would render them unclean, so they refused to give aid.

Who was it that stopped to help the man? A Samaritan, an unclean half-breed reviled by the Jews. The Samaritan went above and beyond simple aid, paying for the man's care long-term. The Jews' enemy demonstrated mercy and love, while the Jewish religious leaders' hearts were hardened. They failed to follow the heart of the law, "love your neighbor as yourself" (v. 27) and justified their failure by the traditions of the elders.

Jesus' critiques continued, as He painted a picture of a prideful Pharisee standing at the front of the synagogue touting how he was not like other people and thanking God he was not like the evil tax collector in the back of the synagogue. In comparison, the tax collector beat his chest, acknowledged his sin, and begged God for mercy (Luke 18:9-14). According to Jesus, it was the tax collector who "went home justified before God. For all those who exalt themselves will be humbled, and those who humble themselves will be exalted" (v. 14). Can you imagine what an offense it would've been to the Pharisees to be presented as less justified before God than a tax collector? No wonder they plotted against Jesus.

The day after Jesus' triumphal entry into Jerusalem to shouts of Hosanna, He went to the Temple courts to teach. The Pharisees came to Him and challenged His authority. Jesus responded with three parables, The Parable of the Two Sons (Matthew 21:28-32), the Parable of the Bad Tenants (Matthew 21:33-46), and the Parable of the Wedding Banquet (Matthew 22:1-14). Each parable makes a similar point.

In the first parable, a father directs his two sons to work in the vineyard. One son says no, but then ends up going to do his work. The other son said "yes, sir," but does not go. Jesus asked the Pharisees, "Which of the two did what his father wanted?" (v. 31). When they replied, "The first" (v. 31), Jesus continued, "the tax collectors and the prostitutes are entering the kingdom of God ahead of you" (v. 31). Ouch!

In the second parable, a landowner planted a vineyard, then rented his land out to tenants. But when the landowner's servants came to collect the harvest, the tenants beat, stoned, and killed them. Thinking the tenants would respect his son, the landowner finally sent to the tenants, but their thoughts turned to taking the land for themselves. So, they killed the son. The Pharisees admitted that the landowner would "bring those wretches to a wretched end" (v. 41). Jesus replied, "I tell you that the kingdom of God will be taken away from you and given to a people who will produce its fruit" (v. 43), and the chief priests and Pharisees realized Jesus was talking about them.

The third parable starts with a king's wedding banquet for his son, but the invited guests refuse to come. The king sends his servants to urge the invited guests to come, but they ignore, reject, and even mistreat and kill his servants. The enraged king deals with the murderers, then instructs the servants to bring in anyone they find, the good and the bad, until the wedding hall is filled with guests.

But the story doesn't end there. The king finds a man in the banquet hall who is not wearing wedding clothes. He binds the man and throws him out into the darkness. Jesus ends the story with, "For many are invited, but few are chosen" (v. 14).

This parable harkens back to the parable about the weeds and wheat growing together and the parable of the ten virgins. All are gathered, the good and the bad, but in the end, the bad will be cast out, and only those in wedding clothes—those with oil for their lamps who are clothed with Christ (Galatians 3:27)—remain.

The Kingdom of God, according to these parables, has zero tolerance for religiosity, hypocrisy, or rejection of His Son. The Kingdom doesn't value the external appearance of things but looks instead upon the heart and measures the person by the attitudes found there. Doing God's will doesn't mean agreeing to follow the ways of Jesus without actually doing so. Doing God's will means embracing His Son in every way. Justice, mercy, and faithfulness are elevated over rigid rule-following or the appearance of righteousness without its fruit.

So, the Kingdom of God is like an innkeeper who brings in many sides of beef to feed his guests. But when he cuts into some of the beef, he finds the insides have spoiled. His inn is well-respected, the highest quality place to stay in the region, so the innkeeper throws out all the spoiled meat, although he takes a great loss to do so, and only serves the highest quality meat to his guests. For in the Kingdom, we "do not work for food that spoils, but for food that endures to eternal life, which the Son of Man will give you. For on him God the Father has placed his seal of approval" (John 6:27).

Ways of the Kingdom

Jesus' parables have unexpected twists because He is describing the counterintuitive Kingdom of God. Look at the Parable of the Lost Son (Luke 15:11-32). The father never behaved in a way we would expect. First, he agreed to give the youngest his inheritance early, which by Jewish tradition should've belonged to the eldest and should've only been given after the father's death. Then, the son squanders the inheritance, defiles himself by working with pigs, and drags himself home unclean. A "good" father would never have embraced this son or allowed him to eat at his table. If this story went as expected, the younger son would've been the villain, thrown out into the darkness.

Instead, the father rushes out to the lost son and embraces him, then not only sets a table for him but has a big party to celebrate his return. "For this son of mine was dead and is alive again; he was lost and is found" (v. 24). In Jesus' story, the eldest son is the villain, the son who's been serving the father faithfully throughout his life, but now grumbles against the younger son, claiming it's unfair that he gets a party.

This parable once again highlights the theme of central importance to the Kingdom of God—love as the motive of the heart. It's also another dig at the Pharisees, who believe they have served God faithfully but whose hearts remain like "whitewashed tombs, which look beautiful on the outside but on the inside are full of the bones of the dead and everything unclean" (Matthew 23:27). The older son's attitude doesn't demonstrate love for his brother; instead, he focuses on protecting his assets and position with his father. In his kindness, the father begs the older son to come into the party, but he refuses.

Other parables of Jesus highlight the theme of seeking the lost at any cost. In the Kingdom, the shepherd leaves the herd of sheep behind in search of the one lost sheep (Matthew 18:10-14), and a widow searches high and low until she finds her one lost coin, then calls everyone to celebrate and rejoice with her over the one coin, something that by worldly standards seems insignificant (Luke 15:8-10). According to Jesus, rejoicing in heaven occurs over each lost soul who comes home (v. 10).

The Kingdom brings in the poor beggar who sat by the rich man's gate, starving, but allows the rich man to enter his own personal hell, because the rich man received worldly comforts during his lifetime, while the beggar received nothing (Luke 16:19-31). When the rich man asks for the poor man's pity, the Kingdom refuses, pointing to the "great chasm" (v. 26) that separates the two men. The chasm was created by the rich man's investment in his own well-being without sharing from the overflow of his abundance. He was selfish and thoughtless toward his fellow man. His own heart left him in his personal hell, where he couldn't receive any help for his agony or send any help to his brothers who stood to suffer his fate.

In the Kingdom, we don't claim places of importance or esteem ourselves above others, nor are we to invite just our friends or rich neighbors to dinner, but we are to invite the poor, crippled, lame, and blind, who can't repay us in kind (Luke 14:7-14). We are to take the last places at the table, "For all those who exalt themselves will be humbled, and those who humble themselves will be exalted" (v. 11). And rather than be repaid on earth, we accept our reward of righteousness in the Kingdom of God (v. 14)

In the Kingdom, faith is highly valued and elicits a response from God. The Parable of the Persistent Widow (Luke 18:1-8) tells how a woman kept hounding an unjust judge until he finally relented. The widow believed in the rightness of her case and refused to give up her faith in justice. As a result, the judge, even though he was unjust, granted her justice. This parable isn't suggesting that God is unjust, but is saying that if an unjust judge will respond to persistent faith, how much more so will our just God? Still, the parable ends with a question. "However, when the Son of Man comes, will he find faith on the earth?" (v. 8).

A similar parable encourages boldness when praying (Luke 11:5-10). A man goes to a friend's house at midnight to ask to borrow bread to feed an unexpected houseguest. The friend complains his door is locked and his children are in bed, but he relents and gives the man the bread he asked for, simply because of what Jesus calls his "shameless audacity" (v. 8).

Jesus ends the parable with the instruction, "Ask and it will be given to you; seek and you will find; knock and the door will be opened to you. For everyone who asks receives; the one who seeks finds; and to the one who knocks, the door will be opened (v. 9-10). He also asks, "If you then, though you are evil, know how to give good gifts to your children, how much more will your Father in heaven give the Holy Spirit to those who ask him!" (v. 13), clarifying what we of the Kingdom seek above all else.

The Kingdom values forgiveness. When Peter asked how many times he should forgive, Jesus answered, "not seven times, but seventy-seven times (Matthew 18:22), tantamount to saying however many times it takes. Jesus then told a parable about a servant who owed a huge debt to the king (v. 23-35). The servant begged the king to forgive his extensive debt, which the king agreed to do out of his merciful heart. But the servant didn't have the same heart. He sought out a man who owed him a pittance and demanded repayment. When the debtor couldn't pay, the servant had the man thrown in prison.

When the king found out what the servant had done, he pointed out the injustice of refusing to have mercy for someone who owed him a debt after his own, massive debt had been forgiven, then the king demanded the servant pay back his debt and threw him in prison, as the man had done to his debtor.

The Lord's Prayer, a short and simple example of how to pray, includes a line about forgiveness: "And forgive us our debts, as we also have forgiven our debtors" (Matthew 6:12). So, in the Kingdom, forgiveness is such a high value that our forgiveness is directly tied to our forgiveness of others. We are to forgive because we have been forgiven so much, just like the servant in the story.

In the Kingdom, worldly treasures have no value. Jesus calls the man who works his whole life to store up more and more things of the world a "fool" (Luke 12:20) because his life is wasted hoarding things that have no value in eternity. By contrast, the Kingdom is of such unmatched value that those who desire it sell everything they own to get it (Matthew 13:44-46).

What Kingdom values do we see in these parables? The Kingdom of God values—and actively seeks—the lost, the poor and those in need. The Kingdom esteems faith in prayer, bold and fervent desire for the Holy Spirit, justice, mercy, forgiveness, and genuine love, while dismissing those things of value to the world, such as wealth, position, status, and even rules and regulations. Rather than looking at the outside of a person, the Kingdom measures by the motives of the heart.

So, the Kingdom of God is like an old, run-down shack standing on valuable land. As long as the ugly shack stands on the land, the value of the land itself is lost. So, the owner of the land will come and tear down the old shack, and build a new, beautiful house, bringing the true value of the property to light.

The Kingdom Made New

The Pharisees once asked Jesus why His disciples weren't behaving like their disciples, or even like John's disciples (Mark 2:18). Jesus' response to them comes in two parts. First Jesus discusses a wedding and fasting versus feasting, saying that while He is here, it is a time for celebration (v. 19). Fasting was associated with mourning, repentance, and spiritual cleansing. As long as He is with them, they have no need to mourn, and as long as they are walking with Him, they have no need for repentance or cleansing.

He also refers to Himself with a new title—the bridegroom—and says when He is taken from them, then they will mourn (v. 20). Given the number of times in the Old Testament where God's covenant relationship with Israel is compared to a marriage, Jesus using this symbolic title is significant. What does this title mean and how does it clarify the answer He gives to the people?

A good example of a similar Old Testament comparison is found in Isaiah 62:4-5 (NET), which says, "For the LORD will take delight in you, and your land will be married to him—As a bridegroom rejoices over a bride, so your God will rejoice over you." The book of Hosea is also filled with marriage imagery—though mostly focusing on Israel's infidelity in light of God's faithfulness—but 2:16 (NET) states, "'At that time,' declares the LORD, 'you will call, 'My husband'; you will never again call me, 'My master.'".

By referring to Himself as the bridegroom, Jesus is declaring He has filled the role mentioned in Isaiah and Hosea belonging to God: husband to the people Israel.

Jesus' prediction that they will fast when He is taken from them calls to mind mourning imagery in passages such as Joel 1:8-9 (NET): "Wail like a young virgin clothed in sackcloth, lamenting the death of her husband-to-be. No one brings grain offerings or drink offerings to the temple of the LORD anymore."

The second part of Jesus' response moves directly into discussing clothing patches and wine storage. "No one sews a patch of unshrunk cloth on an old garment. Otherwise, the new piece will pull away from the old, making the tear worse. And no one pours new wine into old wineskins. Otherwise, the wine will burst the skins, and both the wine and the wineskins will be ruined. No, they pour new wine into new wineskins" (Mark 2:21-22). But what do wineskins and clothing patches have to do with answering the Pharisees' question about fasting? Jesus tells this parable in the same breath as the analogy about the wedding, so He means them as part of a connected idea.

Both the clothing and wineskin analogies focus on trying to put something new and fresh on or in something old and well-worn, and the damage that happens to both if this is attempted. The old and well-worn are the old covenant ways—the ways of the Pharisees, the ways of continual sacrifice of goats and lambs as coverings for sin, the ways of ritual cleansing and rigid laws without consideration of the heart, the ways of burnt offerings and religious festivals, the ways of power and dominance, the ways of hierarchy and control.

Jesus answers the Pharisees' question by addressing the thought process *behind* their asking. They are not really asking Jesus about fasting practices. They are asking Him, "Why don't you do things the old way?" Jesus answers this question behind their question by saying, "I am fulfilling God's role as bridegroom, and you can't expect the new paradigm that I represent to fit into your old preconceptions without both the old and new covenant becoming useless. You need to change your ideas about what a 'marriage' to God means."

Jesus came to bring something new—a new covenant, a new understanding of the Kingdom of God, and a new revelation of who God is and what He values in the form of Jesus Himself. He provides something else new—the Holy Spirit to guide your steps into love, righteousness, justice, mercy, and faith. He came to set you free from bondage, pull you out of hiding, restore you to your original, created identity, and partner with you as your bridegroom to usher in His Kingdom on earth. He came to proclaim love as the highest Kingdom value and demonstrate God's love in a tangible, visible way, through the ultimate sacrifice. "And by that will, we have been made holy through the sacrifice of the body of Jesus Christ *once for all*" (Hebrews 10:10).

Consider This

1. In what ways has entering the Kingdom life been the upheaval of all you've known before? What elements in your life still need to be shifted to the Kingdom life?

2. I describe the Parable of the Sower as the Kingdom Key. What did this parable unlock for you in understanding the Kingdom of God?

3. What evidence have you seen of the "birds of the air" from the Mustard Seed Parable nesting in the "branches" or the "yeast" mixing in with the "dough"? (This can be in the body of Christ or in your own life). In other words, what ways have you enmeshed the Kingdom of God with the realm of the enemy?

4. I describe the "end of the age" prophesies as occurring on many different levels—after Jesus' resurrection, at our deaths, in our hearts when we accept Jesus, and at the coming of Christ again. What are your thoughts on how the "end of the age" parables address each of these different types of endings?

5. Assess the "oil" you have for your "lamp." What do you need to do to prepare for the bridegroom's coming?

6. In what ways have you acted as if God is a "harsh taskmaster" like the last servant in the Parable of the Bags of Gold?

7. I discuss how God has entrusted us with our true nature as a gift. How are you hiding your lamp (your true nature) under a bowl or bed? What beliefs keep you in hiding? Have you noticed a sense of loss or disconnection from your true nature as you've been in hiding? How would you assess your level of trust in God?

8. What feelings are stirred up in you when you read about those who will be thrown out, cast into the fire, or left outside the door at the end of the age?

9. Jesus criticized the Pharisees for honoring God with their lips while their hearts were far from Him and for elevating the traditions of man above God. Have you seen examples where either you or others have given lip-service to following Jesus but failed to demonstrate any fruit? Have you seen evidence of the traditions of man outweighing God's leading in your life or in the church?

10. What are some examples in your life of demonstrating mercy toward others, like the Good Samaritan? In what ways have you been like the priest and Levite toward those in need?

11. What do you think of the father's behavior in the Parable of the Lost Son? Do you think you would've behaved as he did in that situation?

12. What feelings do you notice as you read about the Rich Man and Lazarus? Who do you relate to more? What are your thoughts about the end of that story?

13. I describe how the Kingdom of God values faith and boldness in prayer. How do your prayers demonstrate faith and boldness?

14. For you, what is the most difficult thing about forgiving someone who has wronged or harmed you? How do you feel about Jesus' parable about the consequences of the failure to forgive?

15. Where in your life have you tried to sew a new patch onto old clothing or pour new wine into old wineskins as it relates to your understanding of God's Kingdom?

CHAPTER SIX
PILLARS

We've seen through Jesus' parables how He has come to establish something completely new within us and in the world. It stands to reason, then, He wouldn't use old materials and old methods to build our Kingdom dwelling. "And the one seated on the throne said, 'Look! I am making all things new'" (Revelation 21:5). As God told the Israelites regarding how they were to live in the Promised Land, "You must tear down their altars, shatter their sacred pillars, burn up their sacred Asherah poles, and cut down the images of their gods; you must eliminate their very memory from that place. You must not worship the LORD your God the way they worship" (Deuteronomy 12:3-4 NET).

All of the old things we've worshipped must be torn down. All the things we've used to hold ourselves up and try to keep ourselves safe must be shattered. All the worldly idols we've worshipped must be burned up. The images we've created of ourselves—the façades and masks we've designed to be pleasing and acceptable to others and the pretense we've adopted to try to feel good about ourselves—must be cut down. Even the memory of the "God" of self must be eliminated. The old must be gone, because the new is here (II Corinthians 5:17).

Jesus uses all new ways when building our Kingdom dwelling. We know the new foundation He sets for our dwelling is His Spirit in unity and oneness with our spirits. We've discussed His choice of materials, and how He throws out our old ways and our old beliefs, replacing them with truth as His building blocks. But what holds the dwelling up? What supports the structure so the building can stand? When difficulties arise and storms assail our dwelling, what does Jesus use to steady us?

When times get tough, we often go "back to baseline," meaning going back to old and familiar ways we've used in the past for survival. We might rely on old pillars—those old ways "sacred" to us—to hold our dwelling erect and keep it stable. For example, we might return to the law as well-established pillars to guide our pathways, believing again we can somehow follow the law through our own efforts, and through those efforts ensure our well-being. We may resort to the old ways of trying to earn God's love by being "good enough" to be acceptable to God or trying to "buy" our way into the Kingdom through "good works" as we define them. We could run ahead of God on the path, believing we know what to do and can handle things on our own, or thinking our own knowledge can save us. We may turn back to self-protection or self-judgment instead of relying on Him to be our judge and shield, not remembering that anything of self is rooted in the sin of Eden. We might lean on our own understanding (Proverbs 3:5) instead of trusting in the new ways of the Lord. However, these are not the pillars God provides.

Jesus anchors His Kingdom dwelling with three pillars: Love, Freedom, and Faith. When we live within the boundaries of these pillars, our life reflects the Kingdom of God into the world. The nature of those three pillars act as guideposts for us along the journey. They support us when circumstances bring heavy loads for us to bear. So, let's anchor ourselves in Jesus' new ways by looking in depth at each of the pillars of our Kingdom dwelling.

Love

The example of love anchoring our dwelling is the love displayed on the cross, the *sacrificial* love of Jesus. This love says, first and foremost, "My Father...not as I will, but as you will" (Matthew 26:39). When we walk in step with the Holy Spirit, we "walk in the way of love" (Ephesians 5:2), offering the sacrifice of our whole selves to God.

To walk in the way of love, we must know what love is and how it behaves. We can witness love by observing Jesus, the way He lived, the choices He made, and His actions and responses toward others. We can experience love by how He interacts and responds to us in relationship. And we have I Corinthians 13 as a measuring rod by which we test our actions and attitudes.

Revisit for a moment the key parable, the one by which we understand all other parables. If you recall, the Parable of the Sower revealed the secret of the Kingdom, that the Kingdom is found in the heart, and Jesus came to unite your heart with God. We've seen repeatedly how this unity plays out in partnership and oneness as we make the journey to our Kingdom home. This oneness—this partnership—is the image of love for us to follow.

Just as Jesus came to meet us where we were, we are to meet people wherever they are. We are to come alongside them as He comes alongside us. We are to approach them with empathy, listen more than speak, seek understanding, and respond with truth *as we are led by God.*

The way of love removes any type of relational economy. Quid pro quo is off the table. Love is freely given, with no expectation of return, just as Jesus gave Himself freely to us, not knowing if we would choose to receive His gift, and certain we have nothing to offer Him in repayment. To love like Jesus means to give freely and sacrificially from our hearts out of a desire to give, without demands of return or expectation of benefit to ourselves beyond the fulfillment of our desire to give. "Freely you have received; freely give" (Matthew 10:8).

But this type of sacrificial love isn't produced by our efforts. We can *try* to love, but our human attempts will fall short. An inner transformation of our hearts—our motives, values, and beliefs— must take place before His love can flow from us toward others. And our first act of sacrifice, by necessity, is letting go of our desire to be our own God. Only when we relinquish the sin of Eden through Jesus' transforming presence can we truly open are hearts to others in love.

We are to open our hearts to those around us as He gave Himself freely to us. But, as Jesus instructed the disciples and demonstrated with those who rejected Him, we are to allow those who do not welcome our love or receive it to walk away. In addition, we are to "shake the dust off" our feet if they don't receive us (Mark 6:11), meaning we don't carry any burden of responsibility for their choice. As Jesus knows all too well, we can't force others to receive love. Everyone is free to choose in God's Kingdom.

We also have the Parable of the Good Samaritan, which Jesus shared to describe what it means to love your neighbor as yourself and answer the question, "who is my neighbor?" (Luke 10:29). Based on this parable, someone who loves their neighbor as themselves is helpful to someone in need, makes sacrifices for the good of the neighbor, makes sure their needs are cared for, and goes the extra mile. Someone loving their neighbor is generous, kind, patient, understanding, positive, and loyal. They persevere no matter the hardship caused by helping their neighbor. They think of their neighbor's needs first and serve them willingly, without grumbling or regret. They are forgiving of their neighbor's flaws.

Be careful you don't turn this description into a list of "to do's." Love that doesn't flow genuinely from the heart will not bear good fruit, no matter how "righteous" it appears, for the root—in other words, the motive of the heart—determines the fruit (Matthew 7:16-17). The attitudes of the heart listed—sacrifice, generosity, patience, kindness— flow from you naturally when Christ dwells within you as your partner. Your motive to love isn't obligation or duty but genuine desire. If this isn't the case for you, your focus needs to return to the transformation of your heart, growing your relationship and connection with Him, and building up your internal Kingdom dwelling, for those are the things that will produce the fruit of love.

One unique characteristic of love Jesus demonstrates is the ability to see beyond the surface into the deep places and recognize the true spirit in each individual. And once He identifies the created nature of the person, He treats them according to this identity instead of responding to them according to their lies or sin nature. Like so many things, we will need the help of the Holy Spirit if we are going to pull this off, because we simply don't have eyes to see deeply into someone else without the Spirit enlightening our spirit.

Jesus demonstrated a life where every choice He made was from the heart of love. Even His confrontations with the Pharisees were motivated out of love for them, pointing out their deceptions and lies to try to pull them out of their bondage. We, too, need to mirror His motive and make every choice from the heart of love.

Unfortunately, we don't always know the loving thing to do. It's easy for us to be deceived into pursuing self-benefit over the loving choice, so to follow His example, we need Him to reveal and help us understand the motivations of our hearts that inform our choices, and then to align the motivations of our hearts with truth. With each choice, we check with Him to make sure we are doing the loving thing in truth, and we follow His guidance every step along the journey.

Freedom

The foundational premise, "It is for freedom that Christ has set us free" (Galatians 5:1), anchors our understanding of our freedom in Christ. Our freedom begins with Jesus setting us free from bondage to sin. We are also set free from the constraints and judgments of the law, for, "there is now no condemnation for those who are in Christ Jesus, because through Christ Jesus the law of the Spirit who gives life has set you free from the law of sin and death" (Romans 8:1-2). We are now free to choose to walk by the Spirit in our hearts rather than trying to follow a set of regulations and rules for our behavior.

Once again, we see the secret of the Kingdom evidenced in these verses. *The Kingdom is found in the heart.* We can't create the Kingdom of God through our external actions. No matter how "good" our actions, they aren't able to change our motives. "For it is from within, out of a person's heart, that evil thoughts come…and defile a person" (Mark 7:21, 23).

According to Proverbs 16:2, "motives are weighed by the Lord." We also see in Jesus' teachings on murder (Matthew 5:21-22) and adultery (Matthew 5:27-28) that He is looking upon the motives in the heart, not our behavior. Righteousness only comes through the Spirit, and "The only thing that counts is faith expressing itself through love" (Galatians 5:6).

Paul describes the old covenant as a "veil" that covers the hearts of those who remain under it (II Corinthians 3:15), but "where the Spirit of the Lord is, there is freedom" (v. 17). We now view God's glory with "unveiled faces" (v. 18) so that we may be *transformed* into the image of Christ. The heart—our internal state of being, not our external actions—is what must be transformed. Our actions then flow from the changed heart.

The Jews believed they were free, having been set free from slavery in Egypt. Jesus pointed out their freedom was external only, saying, "everyone who sins is a slave to sin" (John 8:34). He goes on to say, "if the Son sets you free, you will be free indeed" (v. 36).

Free will (the freedom to choose) has always been a part of God's Kingdom. Adam and Eve's free will to choose to listen to the lies of the enemy and try to be like God set slavery to sin in motion. It seems like it would've been better if God had simply made us creatures without will. Wouldn't that choice have prevented the problems that sent Jesus to the cross? Yet, God created us to be free. So, why is freedom so important—important enough for Him to die to secure?

Our ability to give and receive love is based solely in our freedom to choose. The two pillars of freedom and love are inextricably bound. As I discussed, the kind of love Jesus demonstrated—the love of God—is freely given. It flows from choice. Without choice, there is no love, because mandated or controlled love isn't love at all. God's very nature is love, so of course His Kingdom would have the ability to choose at its core, and His creation made in His image would also be given the freedom to choose.

God knew what creating us with the freedom to choose would mean. He put love above all else, as is His nature, and gave us freedom, all the while knowing what would happen. That's how important freedom and love are to Him. The cross loomed before Him, and still He chose love and freedom.

Christ's choice to go to the cross according to God's will has set us free. Each of us must choose to receive God's gift of freedom or to reject it. Sin impinges on our freedom, which makes it opposed to the Kingdom of God. Now that we've been set free from bondage to sin, it's important for us to choose to walk by the Spirit, so that we don't let ourselves "be burdened again by a yoke of slavery" (Galatians 5:1). We are not to use our freedom to indulge our flesh/sin nature, because to do so steals our freedom from us (Galatians 5:13), nor are we to use our freedom "as a cover-up for evil" (I Peter 2:16). Using the cross that set you free to justify doing the thing He set you free from would be "crucifying the Son of God all over again and subjecting him to public disgrace" (Hebrews 6:6).

Living in our freedom is a choice as well. If freedom is important enough to God that He was willing to take on the consequences of our sin for us to have it, we need to protect our hard-won freedom and maintain it against all impositions. Jesus set us free to be whole, to be truly who He created us to be, regardless of our circumstances, and to live according to our Kingdom hearts, motivated by love.

Faith

Faith, the third pillar, is the stabilizing force of our dwelling. It gives the ability to have dimension and substance, for love and freedom without faith are empty and hollow, being produced by flawed human efforts instead of flowing from God. Faith also acts as a shield, useful to "extinguish all the flaming arrows of the evil one" (Ephesians 6:16), and in conjunction with love, a breastplate (I Thessalonians 5:8) to guard our hearts. You might think of faith, then, as the pillar grounding the entrance to our internal dwelling.

Jesus is the "pioneer and perfector of faith" (Hebrews 12:2)—pioneer meaning He tread new ground and discovered new territory of faith, and perfector meaning He completed faith, making it whole and absolute, unspoiled, and all-encompassing. If we want to live out faith, we must be transformed into the image of Christ and live by faith as He did. We must be "crucified with Christ" so that we "no longer live, but Christ lives in" us (Galatians 2:20), for, "without faith it is impossible to please God" (Hebrews 11:6).

Faith is described as "being sure of what we hope for, being convinced of what we do not see" (Hebrews 11:1 NET). The Greek word translated as faith, *pistis,* means persuasion or conviction, and is used in Scripture in the context of belief, trust, justification, and righteousness. Having faith means being fully persuaded (convinced) of what you've heard (Romans 10:17), believing (Romans 3:22), trusting (Romans 4:5), then receiving justification (Romans 3:28) and righteousness, produced from living by the Spirit (Romans 1:17). Do you see how I arrived at my definition of faith as accept (belief), trust (full persuasion), and act (living by the Spirit)?

Faith expresses itself through the presence of Christ dwelling in your heart (Ephesians 3:17), through righteousness (Galatians 5:5), and through love (v. 6). These three witnesses of genuine faith give you "full assurance" (Hebrews 10:22) in drawing near to God.

Faith is not wishful thinking, magical thinking, manipulation, or blind allegiance. Having faith isn't tantamount to crossing your fingers and throwing a coin in a wishing well. Wishful thinking projects into the future focusing on outcomes, but God doesn't focus on outcomes. God focuses on the heart. Faith isn't tentative like wishful thinking. Notice the *assurance* of genuine faith. In other words, faith is what you *know* with certainty, even though your physical eyes haven't seen it. What you know, you know because He has promised it—and your certain knowledge comes through experiencing *Him*.

Faith isn't throwing pixie dust at a problem, either. For example, no matter how "faithfully" you ask, God isn't going to drop a new job at your front doorstep. Will He partner with you to help you find a new job? Of course. He'll encourage you, support you, comfort you, carry you, and love you through the process. That's walking through life with Jesus by your side. He walks through all aspects of life with us. But "believing" for a new job as if the new job is the work of Jesus for you misses the point of the relationship. Our walk with Jesus isn't about what we get from Him in the worldly sense. It's about what He grows in us in the Spirit. As James said, "When you ask you do not receive, because you ask with wrong motives," motives centered on selfish desires or worldly pleasures (James 4:3).

He isn't going to "fix things" for you, either. God is not a "fixer." God is our Redeemer. Yes, He redeems our suffering, as He promised, but that's different from preventing it or fixing it for us. Redemption is bringing good from it, not protecting us from the consequences we've chosen or preventing bad things from ever happening to us. If He was a fixer, the consequences that fell on Adam and Eve in the Garden would never have come.

Neither is faith a way to get what we want from God, as if I could by my faith "force" God to act against His will. Instead, faith is *seeking* God's will for ourselves, because faith means living in the Spirit and walking with Christ. It's the height of hubris to believe I know better than God what would be good in any circumstance. We know how to have relationships based on exchange, with quid pro quo at its base, in this world—although I strongly urge against it—but those types of relationships don't exist in the Kingdom. What is given is offered freely, with no strings attached. It can't be bought, bargained, or manipulated.

Faith isn't holding God accountable as if He owes us. When the fulfillment of His promises is not evident to us, faith is holding onto

Him and trusting His goodness, knowing He has our best interests at heart in all things.

Finally, faith isn't blind. It isn't obedience without question or allegiance without relationship. Jesus has some unkind things to say about blindness in reference to the Pharisees, calling them "blind guides" and pointing out, "if the blind lead the blind, both will fall into a pit" (Matthew 15:14). No, Jesus came so the blind could receive *sight,* not to leave us blind and in the dark.

Paul ascribes blindness to the "god of this age" who "blinded the minds of unbelievers so they cannot see the light of the gospel that displays the glory of Christ" (II Corinthians 4:4). The glory of God is, in fact, the light that emanates from Him, and there is no darkness in Him (I John 1:5). Jesus came to "bring to light what is hidden in darkness and... expose the motives of the heart" (I Corinthians 4:5). Faith sees clearly with spiritual eyes, enlightened by the Holy Spirit, and believes what it sees and knows.

Jesus can handle your genuine questions. He wants your honesty and openness. When we struggle to understand, we can go to Him and ask whatever our hearts need to know. Be clear, though, that doubt is the enemy of faith, as fear is the enemy of faith. Doubt isn't the expression of an honest desire to know and understand—it's the expression of a lack of trust in who He is. Fear isn't coming to Jesus with genuine questions— it's a hindrance to your acceptance and trust, and an indication of the lack of the assurance required to act on your faith. Again, the *motive of the heart* is what counts here. Are you asking from the foundation of your relationship with a true desire to understand? Or are you disbelieving God and refusing to trust Him or act on that trust? As James said, "faith by itself, if it is not accompanied by action, is dead" (James 2:17).

You've seen how Jesus joins with you to create a solid, strong foundation for your dwelling. Upon that base, He constructs an unwavering shelter, a place where you and He live together and the Kingdom exists for you even now, as you journey toward your heavenly dwelling. He uses three pillars to support this shelter. Christ dwells in your heart through faith, you are rooted and established in love (Ephesians 3:17), and Christ has set you free (Galatians 5:1). Bracketed and supported by these pillars, the dwelling stands firm.

Shelter in the Storm

But what happens to your shelter when suffering or tragedy or loss strikes? Will your dwelling withstand being buffeted by the winds of pain? How do you navigate living the Kingdom life while chaos swirls around you and storms pound against your dwelling? What happens to your Kingdom life when you are hit with grief and loss? How do you walk through traumatic events or tragic circumstances from a Kingdom perspective—for they will come. Living the Kingdom life doesn't preempt these worldly tragedies.

Even though sin has been absolved within us once and for all, sin still holds sway *on this earth*. It infests the land and our physical bodies. God told Adam after he sinned, "Cursed is the ground because of you" (Genesis 3:17). He also said Adam would die and "return to the ground since from it you were taken" (v. 19). The enemy is still the "ruler of the kingdom of the air, the spirit who is now at work in those who are disobedient" (Ephesians 2:2). As long as this reality exists—and it will until Jesus comes again—we will face suffering, trauma, and loss. What does your Kingdom journey look like when suffering comes? How are we to understand death?

Having a relationship with Jesus doesn't preclude suffering—far from it. The presence of sin in this world, our own sin, the sin of others, and the ever-encroaching presence of the "god of this age" (II Corinthians 4:4) make hardship inevitable. In fact, everyone will experience trauma to some degree during their lives. At the very least, every individual in this world will experience grief and loss at some point, because death still has its claws in our physical bodies. Other forms of trauma will also occur, everything from unexpected failure on a test to horrific abuse, and everything in between. So, the question isn't whether we will experience trauma, it is to what degree we'll encounter it.

We know we'll face trouble in this world (John 16:33). We're taught to "glory" in our suffering and allow Jesus to use it to grow and mature us (Romans 5:3-5), but how do we glory when our loved ones are in pain, or our circumstances are untenable?

Many interpret suffering as some kind of "test" from God, brought by God to teach us some form of lesson. Others say suffering is God's will. I don't ascribe to these views, foundationally because I believe God has nothing in common with Satan. Since sin in all its forms and the enemy are behind all suffering, I don't see God's hand in the circumstances leading to suffering. Also, we're told there will be no more suffering in the Kingdom of heaven— "no more death or mourning or crying or pain" (Revelation 21:4)—so clearly, God isn't the author of suffering, or it would continue on in heaven.

Where I see His hand is in walking through our suffering with us and in the redemption of our suffering through His mighty power— and this is the answer to how we glory in our suffering. Jesus doesn't intend for us to pretend the suffering isn't happening. Again, He doesn't seem to be a fan of blindness, pretense, or lying. He isn't telling us to just suck it up and get over it. Glorying in our suffering doesn't mean putting on a happy face in the onslaught of great hardship.

But as the suffering sweeps through our lives like a tornado, bent on destruction, we can glory in His presence as our comforter, our shield, our rock, and our shelter in the storm. God never leaves our dwelling. "God is our refuge and strength, an ever-present help in trouble" (Psalm 46:1). Just as Jesus stood outside Jerusalem and wept for the suffering of His children, He weeps with us and for us. We can glory in the truth that we will never experience hardship alone. And we can glory in the certain knowledge that His redemption *will come.*

We can also glory that our shelter stands firm. Suffering doesn't change who God is, for "Jesus Christ is the same yesterday and today and forever" (Hebrews 13:8). We also know suffering doesn't change who we are. Our identity—our created nature—is established and determined by God, not by our circumstances or our experiences. Our created nature is stable, secure, and unchanging, just as God is stable, secure, and unchanging. Together, we form the strong foundation for our internal Kingdom dwelling. Thus, "the rain came down, the streams rose, and the winds blew and beat against that house; yet it did not fall, because it had its foundation on the rock" (Matthew 7:25).

Our internal Kingdom dwelling gives us refuge in the midst of suffering, a place where we can receive solace, where we can find respite, and where we can be held while we weep. Psalm 27 is a beautiful song about the refuge found in the dwelling of the Lord, who the psalmist says will hide you in His shelter and set your feet high upon a rock. The psalmist wasn't talking about avoiding the suffering. In fact, he talks in the same psalm about being forsaken and oppressed, facing false witnesses with malicious accusations against him, and the wicked advancing to devour him. Sounds like hardship to me!

Yet, he understood that "Whoever dwells in the shelter of the Most High will rest in the shadow of the Almighty" (Psalm 91:1). He had no fear (Psalm 27:1). He remained confident in God's goodness (v. 13), despite his enemies, and he seemed to trust in the certain coming of God's redemption. In his dwelling with God, he found rest for his soul in the midst of great suffering.

Grief is one form of trauma we all share, as did Jesus. Jesus understood death as something to weep over, as He did outside His friend, Lazarus' tomb (John 11:35)—even though He knew He would raise Lazarus that very hour. He wept because death was a horror to Him, a tragedy worthy of tears and mourning. Yet, Jesus also called mourning blessed, because of His comfort (Matthew 5:4).

So, how are we to understand death? We are not to love death, embrace it, or seek it. Because it was a consequence of the introduction of sin into the world in direct opposition to God's will, its presence in the world is to be despised.

Yet, we are not to fear it either, because through Christ, death has been overcome and its "sting" has been removed (I Corinthians 15:54-55). If we fear death, we will also fear life. If we dread death or view it as victorious over us, we have missed the message of the resurrection. Remember, we are citizens of the Kingdom of God, eternal creatures. For us, there is no real death. We know "the gift of God is eternal life in Christ Jesus our Lord" (Romans 6:23), yet we still face the layers of issues dealing with death's consequences in our present lives. How do we navigate this difficult path?

Paul offered a simple view of this complicated question. "Christ will be exalted in my body, whether by life or by death. For to me, to live is Christ and to die is gain" (Philippians 1:20-21). If we face death as a vanquished foe, knowing it has no more power over us, in joyous anticipation of the gain we'll receive when we enter the Kingdom of heaven as Paul had, we can continue to live life in Christ with the love, freedom, and faith He provides. Either way, by our lives or by our deaths, Christ in us is glorified.

Where death deals the worst blow in most people's lives is at the loss of a loved one. Perhaps we can face our own death without fear, knowing with certain faith that we will see Jesus when we go home. But when we face continuing to live life without our loved one, many of us collapse under the weight of the pain.

My husband and I lost our son at 17 years of age after a lengthy, degenerative illness. Our grief journey began that day our pediatrician first sent us to the emergency room. Along the way, we faced nine years without a set diagnosis, watching him waste away without knowing why, then eight more years knowing his death could happen at any time and there was nothing we could do. None of this prepared us for the profound and devastating experience of losing our boy.

In Chapter Two, I talked about the process of attachment and bonding, and how God created us for relationships by making attachment a natural and instinctive physiological process. The biology

for attachment is in place within us before birth. We are neurologically built to form an attachment with our loved ones and with God.

Physics also offers unique insight into the attachment process. Scientists have demonstrated how when two particles interact spatially with one another in a vacuum and are later separated into two different, sealed containers—no matter their distance apart—stimulating one particle produces a correlated response in the other particle. This theory is called quantum entanglement. Einstein referred to the phenomenon as "spooky action at a distance."

In much the same way, when two individuals interact and form a relationship, an exchange of energy occurs between the two. This attachment continues even when the two individuals are separated from one another by distance, because through their 'entanglement' the energy continues to be exchanged. Each individual's brain identifies specific energy as their connection with the other individual. This *attachment bond* can be so strong that even when separated for years, individuals can come back together and resume their connection as if no time has passed. The deeper and more intimate and connected the relationship, the stronger the attachment bond.

However, when death prohibits the usual energy from being exchanged, the survivor's brain continues to send out a signal expecting to find the lost connection. But the connection is severed. Their loved one is no longer in the physical sphere. Instead of connection, the individual finds nothing but dark, hollow emptiness. They send their energy out again and again, but it's as if their energy is being sucked into a black hole. The loss of connection creates physiological and emotional pain.

The severed attachment feels like a part of themselves has been amputated. Just like the experience of an amputated limb, the "phantom" feelings of the connection continue long after the energy exchange has been cut. As their energy is drained into nothingness, the grieving individual begins to collapse in on themselves, as if their very being is falling into that black hole of emptiness.

The pain of loss is related to this severing of attachment. When memories of their loved one rise to the surface or are stimulated by circumstances or environment, the individual reexperiences this process, more energy is drained away, and the internal collapse repeats with each reexperiencing.

Grief is the emotional experience resulting from the loss. When you first experience a loss, as with any physiological trauma, you may feel an initial state of shock. You may struggle with processing the emotions you are feeling and with integrating those emotions and thoughts into your here-and-now experience. Your 'quantum entanglement' may make it difficult to accept the loss is real. You might continue to "catch" yourself thinking of calling your loved one or expecting them to walk through the door. Any or all of these responses are normal, but you won't know what your grief will be like until you live it. Everyone experiences their grief differently.

Because each attachment bond is a unique, one-of-a-kind creation, made by two unique, one-of-a-kind individuals, the loss of that connection produces a unique response in each individual. Although my husband and I both experienced the loss of a son, we describe our grief experience very differently. So, no one—not even those closest to you who are going through the same loss—knows or can understand exactly how you are feeling or tell you how you should cope with your grief. No one shares your experience.

That is, no one except Jesus. His connected presence in your heart means He shares your experience with you. He is a part of your 'quantum entanglement.' And because of His presence, and the fact that He is simultaneously present with the individual you lost in heaven, He can help reconnect you to your loved one. He can help recreate the flow of energy you shared in life. But, like so many things, the process of reconnection takes time.

It can also be a painful process, involving telling stories about your loved one and revisiting memories of your shared experiences, both of which initially stir up your pain. As time goes on, however, your memories become sources of connection for you, and your joy in those shared experiences returns, albeit with a bittersweet taste.

Jesus can also bring you glimpses into your loved one's experiences in the Kingdom, which has been a great source of comfort for me as I realized my son truly got the better end of the bargain. "In his great mercy he has given us new birth into a living hope through the resurrection of Jesus Christ from the dead" (I Peter 1:3). What is this hope? My hope is in the certain knowledge our son is awaiting us in the Kingdom of heaven. Our attachment is not lost, it is temporarily suspended. We will be together again, never to reexperience the pain of separation or the severing of our connection. "We have this hope as an anchor for the soul, firm and secure" (Hebrews 6:19).

Even though a loss through death is for the rest of this lifetime, the loss is still temporary, because when we join our loved ones in heaven, everything will be restored and at the same time made new. Our connection will be complete, only better than before, because we will see them with the eyes of Christ in the wholeness of their created being, with no interference from our lies or their sin nature. And we will be seen by them in the same light. "So we fix our eyes not on what is seen, but on what is unseen, since what is seen is temporary, but what is unseen is eternal." (II Corinthians 4:18).

God cushions our loss, gently catching us and carrying us forward to His redemption. God is our redeemer, as Job states: "I know that my redeemer lives, and that in the end he will stand on the earth. And after my skin has been destroyed, yet in my flesh I will see God; I myself will see him with my own eyes" (Job 19:25-27). Job had *faith* in what was yet unseen. We can look forward to the redemption of God because His ultimate redemption has been demonstrated on the cross and in the empty tomb, and we know He always fulfills His promises. His love never fails (I Corinthians 13:8).

Like the individualistic nature of grief, every redemption will be unique, created by God for the good of that individual. "And we know that in all things God works for the good of those who love him, who have been called according to his purpose" (Romans 8:28). In our son's case, the redemption is in the beauty of his life, his ongoing, profound impact on other people, and how much he taught me—and still teaches me—about relationship with Jesus.

God doesn't leave us alone in our grief. He walks through it with us, shedding His own tears as He did for Lazarus and holding us in His comforting arms, so our tears may fall on His strong shoulders.

The Psalms are full of expressions of grief. Psalm 102 paints a chillingly accurate picture of the grief experience. "For my days vanish like smoke; my bones burn like glowing embers. My heart is blighted and withered like grass; I forget to eat my food. In my distress I groan aloud and am reduced to skin and bones. For I eat ashes as my food and mingle my drink with tears (v. 3-5, 9).

Psalm 42 shows us that grief can be mingled with hope and praise. God doesn't abandon us in our mourning. He accepts our flood of tears, listens as we pour out our soul, and receives our questions with understanding (v. 3-5, 11). He doesn't ask us to silence our grief. Remember how open Jesus was with the Father in Gethsemane?

Psalm 116 shares God's redeeming love in the midst of our grief. "The cords of death entangled me, the anguish of the grave came over me; I was overcome by distress and sorrow. Then I called on the name of the Lord: "LORD, save me!" The LORD is gracious and righteous; our God is full of compassion. Return to your rest, my soul, for the Lord has been good to you. (v. 3-5, 7).

Psalm 22 predicts Jesus' own grief experience, so we might recognize Him, understand what He went through, and know the response of God to His agony. "I am poured out like water, and all my bones are out of joint. My heart has turned to wax; it has melted within me. My mouth is dried up like a potsherd, and my tongue sticks to the roof of my mouth; you lay me in the dust of death. Dogs surround me, a pack of villains encircles me; they pierce my hands and my feet. All my bones are on display; people stare and gloat over me. They divide my clothes among them and cast lots for my garment...he has not despised or scorned the suffering of the afflicted one; he has not hidden his face from him but has listened to his cry for help" (v. 14-18, 24).

Finally, Psalm 23—possibly one of the most well-known psalms, following on the heels of Jesus' death experience—describes the solace of God's presence in our grief. "Even though I walk through the darkest valley, I will fear no evil, for you are with me...Surely your goodness and love will follow me all the days of my life, and I will dwell in the house of the Lord forever (v. 4, 6). I find great comfort in the certain knowledge that my eternal dwelling is and always will be God's home.

If Jesus hadn't carried me through the loss of my son, I don't believe I would've made it through. But what I gained from the experience of His presence with me through the grief journey is a deeper faith—an assurance of the breadth of His love, full persuasion of His faithfulness and trustworthiness, and a vision of His Kingdom as I'd never understood it before.

Unfulfilled Longing

We often carry desires in our hearts that remain unfulfilled in this life. How do we explain why a loving God, who says, "Take delight in the LORD, and he will give you the desires of your heart" (Psalm 37:4) doesn't fulfill our desires in this life? How do we continue to walk in the Kingdom life when our longing remains unrealized? I'm not talking about fleshly wants, like a wish for a new car, or new clothes, or a nice vacation. I'm referring to our deep desires blossoming from our true, created nature. Perhaps you long for love from a parent, a spouse, or a child who has chosen to reject you. Maybe your desire is for something for others, or maybe your longing is based on a desire for love and acceptance, or a sense of value, worth, and purpose. True longings, meaning those deep desires based on the truth of who we are and who God is, are good things, *even if* they remain unfulfilled in our lifetime.

Jesus expressed deep longing. He longed for His children to come to Him and rest in the shelter of His arms. "Jerusalem, Jerusalem, you who kill the prophets and stone those sent to you, how often I have longed to gather your children together, as a hen gathers her chicks under her wings, and you were not willing" (Matthew 23:37). Can you hear the pleading in His words? "Please come to Me; please let me hold you and comfort you and protect you; please receive my love." But they were not willing, and His longing was not realized. Despite His longing being unfulfilled, He continued—and continues now—to long for the same thing. His true heart's desire is still to gather us to Him.

Just like Jesus, sometimes our longings are not realized, whether due to the choices of others, circumstances beyond our choosing, or even our own poor choices. Without the Spirit to guide us, walking on the path He walked where the longing was unfulfilled can be discouraging or feel hopeless. We can easily get caught up in the failings or sin choices of others and fall into the trap of unforgiveness ourselves.

However, Jesus did not lose Himself or forget who He was in response to Jerusalem being unwilling to respond to His plea. He did not abandon His calling. He didn't give up. He didn't shut out those He longed for, turn His back on them, walk away, or stop loving them. He didn't choose to suppress His heart's desire and turn toward something unholy or unhealthy to "fulfill" Him in its place. He didn't hide, deny, or blame. Instead, He continues to pursue the desires of His heart.

In the same way, Jesus wants us to continue to pursue the desires of our hearts, but we need to walk the path of longing with Christ. He longs to fulfill our desires for love, acceptance, value, worth, and purpose through our relationship with Him, but when we look to others or this world to fulfill those desires, our longing will remain unfulfilled. Even if we find a special person to truly love us, their love will be imperfect, and the result will be hurt feelings, leaving us with a sense of longing once more. And if we discover a sense of purpose and value in things we do, those things will be transient and temporary— *hebel*—and our sense of longing will return.

If we try to face our unrealized longings on our own, we may give up on something we truly desire. We may be tempted to reject someone who has disappointed us. We may want to retreat into self-protection, to hide ourselves away from being hurt, or to close and harden our hearts in order to shut out the feelings of a longing unrealized. This is not the example Jesus set for us. He calls us to walk the path of longing all the way to the cross with Him.

What does this mean, to walk the path of longing with Christ? I believe He wants us to share His heart. To fully share His heart and experience Him, we must walk with Him in both joy and difficulty, in both gain and loss.

We are called to love, above all else—to love with His heart, as He loves us, which means seeing ourselves as He sees us, loving ourselves for who He made us to be, and valuing ourselves exactly as He values us. It also means loving others—even if they do not know how to love us. How we love ourselves has a direct impact on our ability to love others. If we are unable to see ourselves through Christ's eyes, how can we see others through an unclouded lens? Remember, to love others means seeing their true, created nature through His eyes and responding to them according to their identity. It means choosing the loving thing to do in every circumstance, by discerning with Jesus what the loving thing is.

To walk the path of longing the Kingdom way, we must walk hand in hand with the One who loves perfectly and allow His love to guide our steps. He will gently lead if you are willing, correcting and sustaining you during those times when your longing is unrealized. We need His help to refuse to suppress or give up on our heart's longing, but we know He is able, because He didn't give up on us.

Consider This

1. What have you used as "pillars" in your life that must be torn down? What idols must be burned up? What old ways sacred to you must be removed? What beliefs from your memories must be transformed, and the old beliefs destroyed?

2. What evidence do you see of the pillar of love in your life? How does it support your Kingdom dwelling?

3. How would you answer the question, "Who is my neighbor?"

4. What evidence do you see of the pillar of freedom in your life? How does it support your Kingdom dwelling?

5. How do you protect and value your freedom to choose?

6. What evidence do you see of the pillar of faith in your life? How does it support your Kingdom dwelling?

7. How would you define faith? What thoughts and feelings are stirred by Paul's definition of faith as being fully persuaded of what you've heard, believing, trusting, receiving justification and righteousness, and living by the Spirit?

8. What are some of the ways you've responded to suffering in your life? During which times of suffering did you feel Jesus' presence walking through the suffering with you?

9. Where have you witnessed the redemption of suffering in your life? What forms have His redemption taken?

10. What thoughts and feelings came up for you as you read my description of grief? What were your reactions to the idea of Jesus reconnecting you to the loved one you lost by being 'entangled' with you both?

11. In what ways has your grief been mingled with hope and joy? In what ways has your grief been redeemed?

12. What are your thoughts and feelings as you think about facing death, whether your own or the death of someone you love?

13. What unfulfilled longings do you currently have in your life? Do you experience hope or discouragement over these longings? How can you share with Jesus in His unfulfilled longing?

14. Where have you sought love, acceptance, value, worth, and purpose? What do you think it would look like to receive these things from Jesus?

15. How do you see yourself? In what ways do you show genuine love toward yourself?

CHAPTER SEVEN
HOME MAINTENANCE

Just like our earthly home, you don't "purchase" the treasure of your dwelling and believe your work is done. Now, you and Jesus have daily upkeep and housecleaning, repairs when something breaks down, and ongoing maintenance to keep your home in order. Any "cracks" where the enemy might try to worm his way into your home need to be shored up as soon as they are recognized. If you're not paying attention, your home could fall into disarray and disrepair. How does Jesus help us with this ongoing upkeep?

Our natural entropy—a law of physics that states systems tend toward disorder and the disorder increases over time—applies to our internal state as well. Left without care, your internal dwelling will tend to fall back to baseline, revisiting old neural pathways and entertaining old, familiar lies.

So, not only do you want to pay attention to the ongoing maintenance of your dwelling place, but you also want to partner with Jesus to continuously update, repair, and remodel it to combat the natural effects of entropy. The evil one looks for the smallest of cracks around a window or in the seal of a wall to seek entry. Any opening will do.

Like an octopus, he snakes his tentacle into any access point and grinds at it, picking it apart piece by piece until he can pry it open enough to sneak some lie belief into your home, where it wreaks havoc. Once inside, the lie systematically wears you down while inviting in other lies, until it's recognized and replaced with God's truth.

The first guideline of home maintenance is to join with Jesus to sweep your dwelling every day, looking for vulnerabilities and access points for the enemy's lies. It's helpful to recall that the enemy has

151

nothing in common with God, so creativity is not in his repertoire. He'll use the same old, stale, worn-out lies he's always used on you, dressing them up in some new packaging.

So, begin your sweep by asking Jesus to reveal the presence of any lies you once believed. Examine your responses to those lies. Are they beginning to feel true again? If so, spend time with Jesus, revisiting truth you know and receiving any new truth you need until the lies no longer feel true. Then, ask Jesus to reveal if the evil one has snuck any fragments of new lies in, attached to your old beliefs. Allow Him to address any additional lies revealed by asking for truth in prayer.

Refresh your knowledge of Scripture on an ongoing basis. "For the word of God is alive and active. Sharper than any double-edged sword...it judges the thoughts and attitudes of the heart (Hebrews 4:12). Also, keep a journal of truth you've received from Jesus and read over it periodically. Pay attention to the themes that arise as you review your writing. Often, patterns emerge, and truths fit together to paint a picture of a larger, deeper, global truth. As you renew your mind, you will be able to test your beliefs and grasp God's will for you (Romans 12:2). Make justice your measuring line and righteousness your plumb line (Isaiah 28:17) as you measure your dwelling place.

"Examine yourselves to see whether you are in the faith; test yourselves. Do you not realize that Christ Jesus is in you?" (II Corinthians 13:5). In other words, test yourself against the presence of Christ in you. Do His words in your heart match your self-talk? Are you agreeing with Jesus or entertaining the enemy's thoughts? Do your attitudes reflect Christ's attitudes? When you discover something that doesn't align with Jesus, reject it out of hand, "fix your thoughts on Jesus" (Hebrews 3:1), and refocus with Him on truth.

When you sweep your dwelling, do you find any unforgiveness clogging up your heart? Holding onto the sins of others against you is no different than those sins being your sins—you now carry those sins inside your dwelling. You now carry the weight of that sin in your heart—a horrible burden to bear.

Forgiveness is not accepting sin, as if the sin against you doesn't matter, nor is it excusing the sin. Jesus is quite clear that every sin is unacceptable because it hurts His children. Remember, He said, "If anyone causes one of these little ones—those who believe in me—to stumble, it would be better for them to have a large millstone hung around their neck and to be drowned in the depths of the sea" (Matthew 18:6). True forgiveness is accepting and trusting the grace and mercy offered through the cross, then relinquishing the sin into the hands of Christ, knowing He is just, and allowing Him to deal with the individual who sinned against you according to His will.

The same is true for unforgiveness toward yourself. Christ has forgiven you for your sins, so in continuing to carry them, you set yourself up as the judge, a position reserved for Christ (John 5:22). Your sin then becomes the sin of Eden, setting yourself up as God and judge, against Jesus' instruction, "Do not judge" (Luke 6:37). Once again, forgiveness is accepting and receiving in your heart Christ's grace and mercy, secured at the cost of His own blood, and trusting His love for you.

In your clean sweep, do you find any condemnation, either toward yourself or of others? In the same Luke verse where Jesus exhorts us not to judge, He says, "Do not condemn, and you will not be condemned" (6:37). Paul also reminds us, "Therefore, there is now no condemnation for those who are in Christ Jesus, because through Christ Jesus the law of the Spirit who gives life has set you free from the law of sin and death" (Romans 8:1-2). Having been set free, do you want to sentence yourself once more to bondage to sin and death? Remember, shame is a lie, but if you live as if a lie is truth, you experience the consequences of that lie, so it's as if the lie *is* true for you. Condemnation is the fruit of judgment. Sweep it out!

In our society, anxiety has become so commonplace, it's accepted as "normal," just a part of life. Some even see anxiety as beneficial in some way, as if being anxious is a motivator or keeps us alert to possible trouble. But Jesus says He gives us His peace (John

14:27). He also tells us, "do not worry about your life" (Matthew 6:25). Anxiety or worry indicates we are focusing on what could go wrong instead of on what is good and right and true (Ephesians 5:9). We are focusing on circumstances instead of focusing on Jesus (II Corinthians 4:18).

In truth, anxiety is just fear, which we know is another lie-based belief. The presence of fear means we believe we are in control. Anxiety arises from facing the reality that we have no control, that control is only an illusion which we try desperately to maintain. As we recognize we have no control, we feel out of control—another lie—so, we redouble our efforts to control. Back and forth we go like a ping pong ball between in control and out of control, the spinning wheel of anxiety.

Love and control cannot occupy the same space at the same time. As long as we believe we are in control and live from the dichotomy of in control/out of control, we cannot be truly loving because control grows out of the self-lie of Eden. None of the tools of control—active or passive aggression, manipulation, hierarchical thinking, oppression, domination, and limitation of choice—can exist in our dwelling when loving as Christ loves us is the foundational motivation of our hearts.

Let's revisit the story of the people of Israel. God set them free from bondage to slavery in Egypt, but their experience of freedom was short-lived. Why? Because of fear.

They feared for their lives ("Was it because there were no graves in Egypt that you brought us to the desert to die? What have you done to us by bringing us out of Egypt? Didn't we say to you in Egypt, 'Leave us alone; let us serve the Egyptians'? It would have been better for us to serve the Egyptians than to die in the desert!"—Exodus 14:11-12). They worried about what they would drink and eat ("What are we to drink?"—15:24; "If only we had died by the LORD's hand in Egypt! There we sat around pots of meat and ate all the food we wanted, but you have brought us out into this desert to starve this entire assembly to death"—16:3). They were anxious when things didn't go like they expected ("When the people saw that Moses was so long in coming down from the mountain, they gathered around Aaron and said, 'Come, make us gods who will go before us. As for this fellow Moses who brought us up out of Egypt, we don't know what has happened to him'"—32:1). They feared difficulty, hardship, suffering, and pain ("We can't attack those people; they are stronger than we are...If only we had died in Egypt! Or in this wilderness! Why is the LORD bringing us to this land only to let us fall by the sword?"—Numbers 13:31, 14:2-3).

Time and time again, God demonstrated His faithfulness, and the people responded with fear. And because of fear, they wandered in the wilderness for the remainder of their lives.

What bondage do you keep returning to because of fear? What anxieties do you accept as "normal" parts of life? What worries tempt you to move forward without Jesus? What idols do you cling to because your expectations are not fulfilled? What "giants" in your life do you address through avoidance instead of reliance on God?

As you sweep your dwelling, ask Jesus to show you if you are seeking a false peace or false security through fear and control. Ask Him if fear has caused you to create a false sense of identity—a mask to show others—or to build walls to block others from seeing your true nature. Check with Him to see if worry has you are relying on yourself to achieve righteousness through your own efforts.

Paul offers specific instruction about anxiety. "Do not be anxious about anything, but in every situation, by prayer and petition, with thanksgiving, present your requests to God. And the peace of God, which transcends all understanding, will guard your hearts and your minds in Christ Jesus" (Philippians 4:6-7). Note he references *every* situation—he doesn't say only be anxious when the circumstances call for it.

So, whether we are facing our version of Egypt's armies or "giants in the land" or a reprieve and respite from battle, whether we are experiencing famine or abundance, when we are waiting for God and when we are contented, when we are suffering and when things are comfortable and easy for us, we are to go to God in prayer with thanksgiving. The resulting promise is the peace of God acting as a guard and shield over our hearts and minds through Christ.

In addition to testing the thoughts and attitudes of your heart, we're instructed to check ourselves for self-deception by testing our actions. "If anyone thinks they are something when they are not, they deceive themselves. Each one should test their own actions (Galatians 6:3-4). The adage, "What would Jesus do?" is trite and overused these days, but its principle holds true. Check your actions against the actions of Jesus. Remember to pose the question I suggested earlier in the book: "What is the loving thing to do?"

But, when you pose the question, be sure you listen for Jesus' answer and not your own. Only He can accurately tell you what would be loving in any given situation. Remember, as we discussed, our views of love are distorted by the lies we believe and our own, often wounding, experiences that were misidentified as love or misinterpreted by us as loving. If we listen to our broken conceptualization of love, what flows from us may not be at all what Jesus would do. Ask to see others through His eyes as you seek from Him the loving thing to do.

We also need to check the motives of our heart and sweep away any false motives that arise in us. Is our love motivated by self or the Spirit? For example, is our service of others for their sake, or are we seeking after our own esteem or recognition? Do we "pray standing in the synagogues and on the street corners to be seen by others" (Matthew 6:5) or do we pray in private, seen by our Father alone? (6:6). Do we rationalize our actions and justify them as beneficial for others when they are actually motivated by our own needs? Do we choose our actions based on what makes us feel better about ourselves? The actions don't need to change in these instances—our motives need to be swept clean.

Finally, we are told to test every spirit to see whether the spirit is from God (I John 4:1). Do you recall the image of the sword cleaving the field? The point of that image was the absolute division between the

Kingdom of God and the realm of the enemy. If the spirit you sense has any quality, construct, or connection to evil, it is not of God. Walk away. "Do not quench the Spirit...hold onto what is good, reject every kind of evil" (I Thessalonians 5:19, 21-22). Stand firm against the tactics of the evil one, resisting his deceptions with God's help (Ephesians 6:14).

Invasive Usurper

In the South, we have a problem plant species called kudzu. The plant is native to Asia and Southeast Asia, and as such is not indigenous to the United States, but it currently flourishes throughout the southern region. Kudzu is an invasive, dense vine that grows so rapidly, it overtakes anything in its path, smothering other plants and blocking all access to sunlight, ultimately killing them. The vine will even consume houses.

Seeing a mass of vines draped over trees and hillsides, you might think thousands of kudzu plants overgrew that area, but you are most likely looking at a single plant. Kudzu grows from one taproot. The only thing that kills the kudzu is finding the main root and destroying it. You can try to keep trimming back the vines, but they simply spread and overrun the area again. You can try spraying the leaves, but as long as the root remains, the vine will regrow.

The sad truth is kudzu was invited into the US. Touted as effective erosion control, we welcomed its presence without fully understanding the consequences. Now that it's here, we can't seem to rid ourselves of it or its deadly, oppressive effects.

In many aspects, the enemy is like spiritual kudzu for your dwelling. He is *invasive,* snaking his way into your heart in the form of lies. Once he has a foothold, he spreads his presence into every room of your dwelling and grows his filth well beyond your property line.

He is *not native* to your nature—in fact, he is in every way opposed to who God created when He made you, covering up and smothering your nature, cutting it off from the light and preventing it from being seen by others.

Like kudzu, the enemy enters through one root lie, the lie that you can be God over your own life—the sin of Eden. He spreads other lies—fear, shame, blame, judgment, unforgiveness—but at the heart of it, when you tear everything else away, you'll find the one taproot feeding the whole invasive structure. And like kudzu, killing off aspects of the whole but leaving the root means his presence is still invited, and the lies will return with a vengeance when you get under stress or during times of difficulty.

The enemy is *destructive,* killing and destroying everything in his path. Like kudzu, though, he must be *invited.* He cannot enter your dwelling without permission. The permission can come from you, or it could've been offered by the generations before you and passed down to you. If his presence is generational, the stifling consequences of his presence grow with each new generation unless someone stops the perpetuation of the lie, just like kudzu takes over a whole area if left unchecked.

Satan is also a *usurper.* In the same way kudzu steals the light and nutrients from the plants it overgrows, the enemy steals the authority God gave you over your life and the freedom Jesus provides you by His death. He sucks the life out of you, leaving you feeling depleted, like a shell of who you truly are. Then, he encourages you to invite other, equally destructive things into your life under the guise of filling the void—only you discover at the end of it that it's just more of the same—more kudzu.

The evil one also disguises his lies as desirable, helpful, reasonable, inevitable, and simply a part of life. He doesn't make his tactics or his ultimate goals apparent, or they wouldn't work on us. If we recognized his ways and knew the consequences of agreeing with him, we would rip out that root and crush it underfoot.

Instead, he uses our spiritual blindness against us. He takes elements of truth—much like Satan quoted Scripture out of context when he tempted Jesus in the wilderness—and twists and perverts them to his ends. If we aren't vigilant, he'll sneak his way in before we recognize his presence, and he'll overtake our dwelling, leaving us blanketed with a seething, monstrous growth which masks our true selves and smothers our God-given light.

Taking a Stand

Our physical senses dominate our perception of reality, so it's easy to forget we are in a pitched battle against spiritual forces seeking to destroy us. Complacency is our enemy in this battle. If our physical eyes could see the spiritual reality, we would take our position as a soldier in God's army more seriously. Yet, we are warned about the battle and told we need strong armor to battle the spiritual forces of evil in the heavenly realms (Ephesians 6:11-18).

Paul begins his discourse on spiritual warfare with a challenge, which is really a directive on how to live our lives—"be strong in the Lord and in his mighty power" (Ephesians 6:10). Note Paul's unstated warning about standing against the enemy in our own power. The evil one is a spiritual being, capable of more cunning and guile than we can possibly overcome on our own. Our primary focus, therefore, must be on strengthening our relationship with Jesus, for His presence and strength will be our foundational weapon in the spiritual battle, as His power is made perfect in our weakness (II Corinthians 12:9).

We must remember our battle is "not against flesh and blood, but against the rulers, against the authorities, against the powers of this dark world and against the spiritual forces of evil in the heavenly realms" (Ephesians 6:12). We fight not only for our sakes but for the sake of the Kingdom of God against the invading forces of the enemy.

We also must remember we do not fight alone. Jesus fights alongside us, and our weapons are the weapons of His Spirit. Just as David called on the Lord to fight his battles when he prayed, "Contend, LORD, with those who contend with me; fight against those who fight against me. Take up shield and armor; arise and come to my aid" (Psalm 35:1-2), we are to take our stand with Jesus against the enemy's schemes as the Lord fights the battle.

Since Satan isn't creative—remember, he has nothing in common with God, who is the Creator—his tactics are predictable and consistent. His goals are twofold—convince us our choices are limited so he can squelch our ability to give and receive love and persuade us to hide our true identity to render us ineffective for the Kingdom. The enemy has no real power—notice how he requires our participation and agreement to accomplish his goals—yet his decimation of our dwelling is swift once he gains access, always at our invitation whether we consciously realize it or not.

Our warfare doesn't need to take the form of praying against certain conditions in our lives or for special outcomes we desire. These prayers miss the point of warfare. God didn't provide us with weapons and armor to manipulate circumstances for our benefit. The purpose of our armor is to defend our heart, God's dwelling place within us, and to take back territory from the enemy, reclaiming the world for God's Kingdom. These are our battlelines.

"The weapons we fight with are not the weapons of the world. On the contrary, they have divine power to demolish strongholds. We demolish arguments and every pretension that sets itself up against the knowledge of God, and we take captive every thought to make it obedient to Christ" (II Corinthians 10:4-5). Demolishing strongholds. Obliterating arguments and pretense. Defending the knowledge of God. Capturing thoughts to bring them in line with Jesus. Soldier, these are your orders.

How are we empowered by God to fulfill these orders? II Corinthians 4:7 is clear that we have all-surpassing power, and that this power is from God. Therefore, "We are hard pressed on every side, but not crushed; perplexed, but not in despair; persecuted, but not abandoned; struck down, but not destroyed." (v. 8-9). God provides for the continuation and perseverance of our spirit in the battle.

The enemy wants us to believe we are overpowered and overwhelmed, like an untethered boat in a hurricane, caught in the pitch and swirl of the wind and waves crashing against us. He tries to confuse us with distortions based on our past experiences or our present circumstances, with a goal of perverting our view of God's character and our own identity. He tempts us to "drink the sea water"—which, as any sailor will tell you will kill you, and quickly—even though fresh, living water is always available to us.

But the truth is we are well-equipped for the fight. The weapons we need—and the eternal things that sustain us—are given to us by God. "Therefore we do not lose heart. Though outwardly we are wasting away, yet inwardly we are being renewed day by day. For our light and momentary troubles are achieving for us an eternal glory that far outweighs them all" (v. 16-17).

One of our most important stances against the enemy involves our identity. Are we being fully and completely who God created us to be? Are we expressing our nature and allowing that nature to flow freely into the world? God created us to be exactly who we are, so being anything else leaves a hole where we were meant to stand. But simply being who we are pushes back against the enemy, through the nature of God expressed in us and through us. In that sense, we don't *do* anything in the battle—we stand by *being*. As Paul described, "after you have done everything, to stand" (Ephesians 6:13).

Do you see yourself as a warrior for God's Kingdom? If you don't believe you are part of the divine battle, or think you have no strength or power to fight, ask Jesus to reveal the truth to you. Everyone has a role to play, and you can't sit out this war. If you try to opt out, your Kingdom dwelling will be diminished, and the coming of the Kingdom of God will be hindered by the gaping hole you left on the frontlines.

House Guests

How do you navigate relationships with those who are not of the Kingdom of God? And how do you walk alongside those who are also on the journey? How do you decide who and what to allow entrance beyond your Foyer? And what happens if someone or something gets in that later proves false? How do you banish them and repair the breach?

Trust is a particularly difficult path to navigate. We've already established the importance of trusting Jesus, but what does He say about trusting others? We are told love always trusts (I Corinthians 13:7), but Scripture also acknowledges that not everyone is trustworthy (I Corinthians 4:2, I Timothy 3:11, Titus 2:10). Jesus taught several parables about trustworthy servants, with the message, "Whoever can be trusted with very little can also be trusted with much, and whoever is dishonest with very little will also be dishonest with much" (Luke 16:10).

So, it doesn't appear Jesus is telling us to trust indiscriminately. At the same time, if we are to approach someone with a heart of love, we will begin with open arms and a trusting spirit, at least until they prove themselves untrustworthy.

We are told, "do not resist an evil person. If anyone slaps you on the right cheek, turn to them the other cheek also. And if anyone wants to sue you and take your shirt, hand over your coat as well" (Matthew 5:39-40). We are also told to flee from those who persecute us (Matthew 10:23) and refuse to associate or eat with believers who continue to sin (I Corinthians 5:11, 13).

Relationships are hard.

My solution to this knotty issue is to stand on the truth I know—I trust Jesus, wholly and completely. When I am unsure whether to invite someone to enter my dwelling—in other words, to trust them—I ask Jesus and trust He will guide me in the right way to go. That way, I am relying on Jesus instead of on humankind (I John 4:16).

Regarding what *things* we bring into our dwelling place, Scripture is quite clear. "Resist the devil" (James 4:7). "Flee from idolatry (I Corinthians 10:14). "Do not let sin reign in your mortal bodies" (Romans 6:12) or "offer any part of yourself to sin as an instrument of wickedness (v. 13). The bottom line is we are not to allow anything of the evil one into our Kingdom dwelling.

Notice that each one of these instructions contains an action verb. Resist, flee, do not let, do not offer. I mentioned before how Jesus constructs our dwelling walls with the built-in protections of truth and peace. We are called to stand on His truth and live in His peace as partners with Him, to protect our dwelling and guard our heart and mind.

Our physical senses are once again a problem for us here. We observe the appearances of things in the world, and those observations often have more influence on our responses than the truth of Christ. We allow circumstances to affect our peace more than we allow His presence to sustain it. In moments of difficulty, we tend to forget the truth He's told us, and we quickly let go of our peace and pick up fear.

With God's help, we can choose to value truth over the perceptions of our senses. We have plenty of evidence that senses can give an inaccurate view of things. For example, our living room is painted a lovely pale color, but every time it's mentioned, my husband calls it green, and I call it blue. Our perceptions of the walls are very different. Which one of us is right? There's no way to know.

Paul talks about how we perceive through an obscure image (I Corinthians 13:12). Jesus said, "Although they see they do not see, and although they hear they do not hear nor do they understand" (Matthew 13:13). This was certainly true even of the disciples, who misperceived Jesus' ministry all the way to its end. If we are fully persuaded and accept our senses are untrustworthy receivers, distorted and perverted by many factors, including the lies we believe, perhaps then, we will give more weight to Jesus' truth.

One thing we have going for us is the truth is always true. Nothing changes it—not circumstances, not opinions, not feelings or thoughts, not trauma or suffering, not loss, and not outcomes, whether desirable or undesirable. It isn't distorted or perverted by our perceptions. Truth is not *hebel.* Jesus Himself is the truth (John 14:6), so when we stand on the truth, we stand firmly with Jesus. Through this partnership, we can refuse entry to anything we do not desire within our Kingdom home.

Pouring Out from Abundance

A final issue that needs to be addressed is how and what you will pour out of your abundance into the world. Yes, it's wonderful to share the kind of intimacy and freedom I describe, but if that relationship produces no fruit where it pours light into others, it's no more than another self-focused sham, a counterfeit of what Jesus offers. What has Jesus given you to pour out? As you come to know your true identity, how does that affect what you pour out into others? How does your identity inform how you live your Kingdom life?

A flower sends out its seeds naturally. They flow from the flower and fall where they may. The flower doesn't water them, fertilize them, or tend them. They grow simply from the flower being the flower. And we know what will grow from the seeds based on the nature of the seed sown.

The same is true of us. When we are being our true, created selves, the seeds flow freely from us, just from being who God created us to be. Jesus is the one who determined the nature of our seeds, and He is the one who tends the seeds once they are sown. But if we are not being our created selves and allowing the essence of our nature to flow, Jesus has nothing to tend because nothing is being planted.

Our job is to *be* the flower. God has poured into us in abundance from His own nature. He pours His boundless love into us every day. What a waste if we hoard that abundance inside ourselves and never share it with others. We become, then, like the wicked, lazy servant who buried his gold and returned it to his master without any growth (Matthew 25:14-30). Remember what happened to him? It involved darkness, weeping, and gnashing of teeth.

This parable would also intimate that if we hoard the abundant gifts of God, it means we don't truly know who God is or fully trust Him. The servant believed the master was a hard man and a harsh taskmaster, a demanding exploiter. He hid his gold in fear as a result. If we are hiding our identity, are we believing the same things of God?

In Scripture, the branch that bears no fruit is cut off, and the fruit-bearing branch is pruned so that it bears even more fruit (John 15:2). The fig tree that bore no fruit for Jesus withered (Matthew 21:19), just like the Pharisees, who produced the fruit of hypocrisy, judgment, and exclusion from the Kingdom. "What good is it, my brothers and sisters, if someone claims to have faith but has no deeds? Can such faith save them?" (James 2:14). James is not referring here to doing good "works"—the Pharisees did that—but is referring to the fruit of genuine faith, which is a heart of sacrifice poured out to others. His challenge is to the nature of the so-called faith. His question is, can a faith that isn't true faith (acceptance, trust, and action) really save someone? The answer is no.

To love God with all of our hearts means to live fully and completely from the heart He created within us. It means allowing Him to break the stronghold of the flesh/sin nature, to sacrifice our desire to be our own God, and to allow Him to cleanse away anything holding us back from being fully who we were created to be.

Through His Spirit living within us, we are able to know and live in the fullness and wholeness of our created being. To love our neighbor as ourselves means to allow His love to fill us to the brim, loving ourselves fully and allowing His love to flow freely out into those around us. And the more we allow to flow, the more God pours into us.

The Example We Follow

As we live the Kingdom life, we're not on our own. Jesus set His feet on the path of the Kingdom life as a living, breathing example for us. He also walks with us on the path as our guide, our support, and our comforter. He has "made God known" (John 1:18). According to Jesus, "If you really know me, you will know my Father as well. From now on, you do know him and have seen him" (John 14:7). Just as Jesus only did what He saw His Father doing (John 5:19), we are to do what we know Jesus did—and what we see Him doing now within us.

Jesus didn't fear death, nor did He elevate it. He faced death head-on as a part of the enemy's realm, fought it, and brought it to its end, so that we would never have to experience it. The example He set for us is to live life to its fullest abundance while living in our internal Kingdom dwelling—for what we sow here will come to full blossom in heaven.

Jesus didn't allow the trauma, abuse, rejection, and loss He experienced to define Him or determine His identity, nor did He feel disqualified for or unworthy of love because of His experiences. The example He set for us is to know our identity based solely on who God says we are, ignoring the input of all worldly sources in defining our natures, and to live from the nature created in its fullness.

Jesus didn't get discouraged when His longing was left unfulfilled in this world. The example He set for us is to trust God even when the world around us is filled with chaos and pain and to expectantly anticipate the redemption of God, knowing that He is our Redeemer.

Jesus didn't love others from a sense of His own need, having within Him the fullness of the love of God and being in His nature love. The example He set for us is to love God with our whole selves, allowing His love to fill us, and from the overflow of His love allowing our love to flow into others in the same way that He loves us.

Jesus didn't deny the existence of evil, minimize its impact, or ignore the need to battle the enemy. The example He set for us is to name evil for what it is, recognize the deceptions of the enemy, and fight his lies with the truth of God.

Jesus didn't wait passively for life to happen to Him. He walked intentionally toward His purpose, knowing His goal, and every step He took and every choice He made furthered His goal. The example He sets for us is to make our choices actively with intention and purpose in partnership with Him along the Kingdom path, sowing good seeds to grow into fulfillment in our heavenly home.

Jesus didn't walk alone. He always walked with God. He also walked with others, His disciples and friends with whom He shared His experiences and truth. The example He set for us is to walk in relationship with God and with others, listening always to His truth, and offering support and encouragement to others against the pressures of the worldly perspective and the sin nature.

Finally, Jesus didn't look ahead to the Kingdom of God as a future reality. He brought it! The example He sets for us is to live in the Kingdom of God within us, and to usher His Kingdom into the world through the expression of our God-reflecting natures and the overflow of His love from our hearts.

Bringing It Home

Jesus has been hard at work throughout this book, tearing down your old structure. He has helped you identify your lie beliefs. He has broken through your walls. He has even done a "deep dive" in your heart to go after the sin of Eden, and you've relinquished your death grip on your belief that you can be your own God. As a result, your desire to control has melted away as you accept there is no such thing as control. Your hierarchical perspectives have shifted from vertical to horizontal, so you see everyone, including yourself, on the same plane, equal in value but unique in makeup and purpose.

He has also labored with you to build up your new internal dwelling. Your foundation is set as you and He have become one, like a bride and bridegroom. He's given you truth to shore up your walls. He's flooded your spirit with peace to guard your heart and mind. You know who you are because He's restored your created identity, and you know who He is because you've become intimately connected to Him as your partner. He's opened a space within you where others can come and see your true identity, which now flows freely into those around you.

You find your values have shifted. Where once you were divided between the Kingdom of God and the realm of the world, you have placed your feet firmly in the Kingdom, and your heart desires the

Kingdom way. Fear and shame no longer direct your steps; instead, you rely on the Holy Spirit to be your Guide. You sense your neural pathways are rewiring, too. Your usual, automatic responses—those you would expect based on your prior experiences—are changing. Things that used to engender anger or frustration are now met with love and peace. Things that would've stirred fear are now embraced with faith.

The burden of unforgiveness has lifted off your shoulders, and you feel a sense of freedom you've never felt before, a lightness and a supernatural calm. Colors are brighter. Food tastes better. You feel more alive. You sense Jesus' presence with you at all times, and your connection with Him is strong. You hear and recognize His "voice" as if you are talking to a friend who is in the same room with you. You relish your times alone with Him as a rejuvenating stream of living water, but now you experience Him throughout your days, even in the midst of work or family responsibilities. He has become your true partner.

Or maybe you are somewhere else along the path of your journey. Perhaps you are struggling to let go control. You might still need to forgive someone—or yourself—for a wrong done to you. The sin of Eden may still rear its head in you, particularly when you're under stress. You may be holding onto some of your old ways, clinging to them like a life preserver because you are still uncertain of God's goodness and faithfulness. Your faith may stop at acceptance as you struggle to learn to trust God completely, or you may have difficulty still allowing your faith to flow out into action. You might still be searching for your true identity.

Wherever you are on the path, remember He has gone before you, has been at work in you, continues His work in you, and walks the path with you. Jesus always meets you where you are. "The one who calls you is faithful, and he will do it" (I Thessalonians 5:24). Be confident "that he who began a good work in you will carry it on to completion until the day of Christ Jesus" (Philippians 1:6).

I hope these chapters will motivate and encourage you to continue on your journey, knowing that what I describe is *real* and *possible* for you. You *can* know true freedom. You *can* live in a transcendent peace. You *can* have the type of connection and oneness with Jesus that you desire.

May you follow Christ's example in all ways, walking in oneness with Him as He walked in oneness with the Father, loving as He loves you, and living as He lives within you. And may your Kingdom dwelling—both the internal home He builds with you in your heart and the heavenly home He has gone before you to prepare—be filled to overflowing with all things true, all things pure, all things beautiful, all things wonderful, all things praiseworthy, and all things glorious. And may your journey shine bright with the light of the glory of God.

Consider This

1. What 'cracks' have you noticed in your internal Kingdom dwelling? What tactics does the enemy use to try to gain access?

2. What old lies commonly resurface in you if left untended? What truth counters those lies? What keeps those truths from being grounded and secure in your heart? (Pray about how the enemy deceives you into agreeing with the lies again to uncover what keeps the truth from remaining firmly in place).

3. What overarching themes have you observed in the truth Jesus has shared with you? What deeper global truths have you gleaned from those themes?

4. How do you test your beliefs? Your thoughts? The attitudes of your heart? Your actions? The spirits?

5. What do you need to forgive, both in yourself and in others? What keeps you holding onto those sins?

6. In what ways do anxiety and worry evidence in your life? What are the focuses of your anxiety and worry? What truths replace those fears?

7. What false motives underlie your actions? (Consider the rewards you receive and check if desire for those rewards

motivated your choices). In what places in your life are you more focused on self than on Jesus?

8. Do you see yourself as a warrior for God? What equipping has God provided you for warfare? (Think in terms of the elements that make up your nature and envision those aspects of your identity in the battle).

9. In what ways and in what circumstances have you been tempted by the enemy to "drink the seawater"—in other words, consume what he is offering you—instead of relying on living water from Jesus?

10. What are your thoughts and feelings about trusting God? Trusting others? What are the hindrances to trusting, both God and others?

11. What things have you let into your internal dwelling in the past that you desire to forbid entry in the future?

12. What aspects of your nature have you hidden or hoarded? What aspects of your nature flow easily from you into others? In other words, in what ways is your flower open and sending out seeds?

13. What fruit grows from the overflow of your heart? In other words, what seeds are you sending out?

14. I listed eight examples Jesus set for us in His life. Which of these examples have evidenced themselves in your life? Which examples have you struggled to follow? Which ones stood out to you the most? Which ones struck an emotional chord in you?

15. Where do you see yourself on your journey to your Kingdom dwelling?

ABOUT THE AUTHOR

As an award-winning author, professor, and Christian counselor, I've spent my life helping people with various aspects of mental health, equipping clients, students, families, and yes—even nations in crisis—to tap into who God created them to be, understand how He has wired us as human beings, and discover that the Kingdom of God is within us—always.

My husband, David, and I enjoy working and writing together. Our passion is to help others explore and deepen their relationship with Jesus Christ, and our work and our writings are geared toward that goal.

Our children are grown with families of their own. Our son, Hayden, is a teacher, married to Natalie, a nurse. They have two children, Coen and Petra, our precious grandchildren. Our daughter, Lindsey, is a veterinarian, married to Kyle, an electrical engineer.

Our youngest son, Cody, passed away at the age of seventeen from a degenerative neurological disorder. His life stands as a beautiful reflection of what it means to live in the Kingdom of God within. You can read more about Cody's story at https://codylanefoundation.com.

OTHER BOOKS BY THIS AUTHOR

Fiction

The Interview
Sky Light Falls: Whisperers Book One
Sky Light Rises: Whisperers Book Two
Sky Light Ends: Whisperers Book Three
Coming Soon: This Hallowed Ground

Nonfiction

Wilderness Meditations
Strength in Adversity
Strength in Our Story
Seeking Treasures
Restored Christianity
Dwelling

Professional

Please Share the Door: I'm Freezing—Creating Oneness in Marriage
Trauma Narrative Treatment
Gold Stone

How to Connect

Websites— https://thedoctorslane.com
https://restoredchristianity.com
https://codylanefoundation.com
Facebook— https://facebook.com/dr.donna.e.lane
Twitter—@Doctordelane
Instagram—@doctordelane

Made in the USA
Columbia, SC
09 October 2021